The Resurrected Dead, Now Immortal, Live Among Us

A MANUAL FOR IMMORTALITY

The Resurrected Dead, Now Immortal, Live Among Us
A Manual for Immortality

Sacred Fire Publishing Co.
www.sacredfirepublishing.com
Texas

Booklocker Publishing
PO Box 2399
Bangor, ME 04402-2399
www.booklocker.com
ISBN 1-59113-479-X

Library of Congress Control Number: 2004091554
Library of Congress
Cataloging in Publication Division
101 Independence Ave., SE
Washington, DC 20540-4320

The information in this book concerning diet, health and meditation practices are given as personal experiences of the author and as suggestions for the reader. It is in no way to be considered medical advice. Please seek the advice of your Physician if you have any concerns.

Printed in the United States of America.

The Resurrected Dead, Now Immortal, Live Among Us

A MANUAL FOR IMMORTALITY

Jhershierra

Introduction

It may seem shocking to some, and unbelievable to others, but the truth is: the miracles, resurrection and ascension which Jesus did—we can all do. Jesus said in Matthew 17: *"If you have faith the size of a mustard seed, you will say to this mountain, 'Move from here to there,' and it will move. Nothing will be impossible for you."* This is not some empty promise he made, but a real and achievable goal for humanity. Why is this achievable? Because others have done it and they walk among us as great Immortal Beings.

The message in this book comes from my own personal experience, as well as from revelations I have received while interacting with the Immortals. All the personal experiences are true and are given as examples of the manifestation of these truths. The way I express myself in writing is an extension of my style of teaching, which is candid and straightforward. This will appeal to those who are yearning for a no-nonsense, practical approach to changing their lives.

On a personal note, I am a teacher, not a writer. My creativity and inspiration comes from interaction with others. It is hard for me, as I look at a blank computer screen, to write what comes naturally for me when I teach. I guess this is why it has taken me so long to write this book.

The path to physical immortality and miracle-working requires hard work, determination, and an unwavering commitment to freedom. It is no accident that we are seeing a rise in polarity between the so-called New Age Liberal Left and the Christian Conservative Right. Tensions and chaos are part of the natural process when we are giving birth to a new and better way. It is with the greatest love and desire for humanity's freedom that I present this book to those who are seeking.

In Matthew, Chapter 10:7-8, Jesus gave this command to his disciples, "*The Kingdom of Heaven is at hand. Cure the sick*, ***raise the dead,*** *cleanse lepers, and drive out demons."*

The resurrected dead, now immortal, are living among us.

Table of Contents

Part One

Part One discusses the nature of God and Creation. The beginning of man's existence, his glory and his fall are laid out in a historical account of events.

This section is written in a style reflective of contemplation and study.

In the Beginning

In the beginning was Consciousness. This one Consciousness was self-aware, deep and motionless.

At a time of its choosing, the One moved and became active; creation began. The One was now reflective and resting—active and creating. From this, all that is known became.

Thought encompassed all that was and upon this thought, creation was born. The One's thoughts and creations were limitless and beyond measure, and for eons, the One admired all it had created.

During a time when the One was deep in thought, it became aware of the desire to be with its creations in a more personal way. The One then created the ability to study and explore its creations in smaller increments.

To do this, the One gave birth to individualized aspects of itself. The One now became the "I AM," and its individualized aspects, "THAT I AM."

The I AM was now able to enjoy all of its creations in even more limitless ways by the children it had created. These children were flames birthed from the one Fire. Each Flame had both reflective/resting, as well as active/creating aspects. They were identical to their parent the I AM.

Eons passed, and the Flames produced many wonders. Slowly, as they used their energy over time, they built many complex patterns of thought. In such an act of creation, LIGHT was born. When the Flames saw what they had brought into being, they marveled at its beauty.

The Children of the I AM then began to experiment with, and explore, various patterns of light; soon this light gave way to structure and form. They saw what they had created and were pleased.

After a while, the I AM became full of different structures of light, that which was translucent, as well as that which was dense. Soon universes, solar systems, suns, planets and the like were born.

During a time when the Children were deep in thought, they became aware of the desire to interact with the realms of light in a more personal way. Instead of experiencing all of the realms of light at once, they would create the ability to focus, study and explore these realms in smaller increments.

Thus, the Children gave birth in the realms of light, and as a result, Twin Rays of Light were created. Each Ray of Light was endowed with all the qualities of their parents, but one was predominantly resting/reflective and the other was acting/creative. Duality was born, and, with this new ability, the Children were now able to experience the realms of light in myriad forms and delve deeper into matter.

The physical worlds of creation became an exciting place to be. For eons, the Rays of Light lived and traveled among the various physical creations and enjoyed the freedom to create just as their parents, the I AM Children, did. The Rays always remained connected to their parents, just as their parents remained connected to the I AM.

They produced many wonderful things in the physical worlds. As they experimented with denser levels of light, they would often project their consciousness into these new forms of matter. This experience gave them new sensory sensations and resulted in many different types of physical forms throughout the universe.

As time passed, some of the Rays of Light began to admire the forms they had created, so much, that they stayed in them and did not dissolve them back into unstructured light. When the I AM Children saw their offspring's attachment to these identities, they suggested that the Rays release their forms and try something new. Some of the Rays of Light did, but others, decided they liked this new sense of identity and wanted to keep it. To them, it was an experiment, a journey that took them deeper into Self-discovery.

The Children watched with interest as their offspring moved further from their true identity and deeper into their physical creations. The Rays of Light began to identify more with what they had created than with who they originally were. They began to forget they were ever-changing, ever-expansive Rays of Light, and instead, they began to think of themselves as limited, restricted physical forms. The I AM Children watched with love and patience as their offspring played in their newly limited worlds. They knew that all was in perfect order, because, after all, it was merely the I AM experimenting with itself.

More time passed. Soon these Rays of Light became so isolated and separated from their original identity that they began to think of themselves as unique in the universe. In their isolation, they imagined themselves to be more powerful than any other thing, and they sought to take control over the worlds of physical creation. These Rays of Light became known as the "Separatists."

The Separatists tried to convince other Rays of Light to join them. Many Rays did not choose their path, and the Separatists found it difficult to live in harmony with them. The Separatist Rays aspired to shape everything in their worlds, so this refusal provoked a desire in them for domination.

They tried to assert this domination, but failed, because the Rays of Light were not restricted and confined, so they easily dissolved all they had created in the physical worlds. Thus, the Separatists had nothing to possess and retreated deeper into separation.

Patiently, the Separatists waited until their siblings started to play in physical forms again. Then the Separatists went forth in small groups, rather than as a whole to the new worlds. Slowly, they convinced their siblings of their "superior" ways. Some these worlds began to see the enjoyment of living in a permanent physical body, and the Separatists gained rule over these planets and their siblings. Slowly they succumbed to the new experiment and in their isolation fell into a deep sleep. All that they once were became a memory. A fog of forgetfulness lay across their consciousness without their freer, more expanded siblings to remind them of who they were; they became trapped in their physical form.

Once this fall was complete, they lost their abilities to shape shift, be immortal, communicate telepathically, manifest instantly, and travel the heavens. The density of their physical forms even isolated them from one another. Unable to read each other's thoughts and feelings, as they had done before, they developed new behaviors of suspicion, fear, and survival instincts which crowded out their spiritual abilities.

Their immortality lost, the form they had loved and cherished began to decay and die. A sense of helplessness ensued, and they spent all of their time trying to preserve their bodies and enjoy as much of their physical lives as possible.

The I AM Children, wishing to provide a way for their offspring to regain their sense of identity, established a new direction in the form of laws. They knew that, eventually, the Separatists would get tired of playing in isolation and seek a way out of their limitations.

Their true identity would eventually resurface and the desire to regain immortality and harmony with their siblings would create the opportunity for a reunion to happen.

Throughout this experiment in separation, the I AM gained greater knowledge of itself. It was a grand opportunity for the I AM to experience the ultimate in separating itself from itself in order to feel the overwhelming joy and love of finding itself once again.

Our History

Then God said, *"Let US make man in OUR image, after OUR likeness.... God created man in his image, in the divine image He created him; male and female He created them."* Genesis 1:26-27.

The I AM Children created planet Earth after which they said, *"Let us create aspects of ourselves that can experience physical light and live on this planet experiencing all that matter has to offer."* Using the realms of light, they created Twin Rays of Light in their own image, so their dual nature might have greater freedom. These Twin Rays were male and female, and each was endowed with the consciousness of their Creator. The I AM Children created many of these Twin Rays, and they filled the whole Earth.

The Separatist Rays, seeing how beautiful the Earth was, also desired to colonize there and for a while did not interfere with the Twin Rays. However, after the Separatists became firmly entrenched on Earth, they began to make contact with the Twin Rays and intermingled with them. The Twin Rays were greatly outnumbered, and they made the decision to leave the surface of the planet. Some left and relocated to other planets; others went to higher levels of light. However, a portion of the Rays of Light went deep into the Earth. Living inside her, they created a new world. All that remained on the surface of the Earth were those who delighted in the Separatist body and its sensations.

Left alone, for the most part, the Separatists created a way to produce new bodies using sex organs. Upon death, their consciousness would leave and reincarnate into a new body that was just being born. As time passed, the men and women focused their efforts on creating as many kinds of physical sensations as they could. They explored ways to incite fear; they indulged in gluttonies and pleasures. They abused the body in order to feel the sensations of hunger, pain and disease. They created elaborate ways to stimulate the sex organs, had sex with various other animal forms, and took pleasure in tormenting the creatures of the Earth. War became continuous and great civilizations rose up, only to be destroyed.

Meanwhile, deep inside the Earth and oceans, the Rays of Light thrived and developed an advanced civilization. Because they were still immortal and retained their original powers, they were able to create whatever they wanted from thought and live beyond the limited reality of the surface. Over time, Rays of Light from other planets came to visit. Throughout the galaxy, advanced civilizations developed and worked together in harmony.

Separatists who lived on other planets also developed technology, which allowed them to travel, and wars broke out among the different Separatist planets. Many planets were destroyed, and new ones had to be found. Some of these space-traveling Separatists came to visit Earth.

With the guidance of the I AM Children, the Rays of Light established counsels creating laws and teachings to offer the Separatists options other than the path they had chosen. Many representatives from these counsels met with the Separatists in order to offer a new alternative. Some even incarnated into the Separatist bodies in order to teach them in a more personal way. Most of them succumbed to the sensations of the body and lost their immortality. Those that did not succumb either went into the immortal cities inside the Earth or returned home in Light vehicles (space ships).

The Counsels occasionally tried to interact with the Separatists, but because Earth was such a beautiful planet, it became the planet of choice; many different sects of Separatists colonized and fought for control. The Rays of Light, who had originally come to help humanity, left behind their teachings hoping that, one day, the Separatists might want to seek freedom from their situation.

Over time, there was an acceptance of these teachings by some, and this made other Separatists fear losing power. The Separatists decided to create teachings of their own and threatened anyone who did not follow with a horrible punishment. Those who supported the Rays of Light's teachings took them underground, and they continued to flourish. After ages had passed, many of the Separatists began to feel the oppression of their physical forms. Displeasure began to outweigh the pleasure, and the long forgotten memory of who they were slowly began to resurface. This development encouraged the Counsels to send more support to Earth. The Counsels recognized that if enough Rays of Light—along with enough Separatists—desired a new reality, then change on a large scale might be possible.

As time passed, the teachings by the Rays of Light grew in popularity. Even though infiltrators who sought to hide or distort the truth had corrupted much of the original teaching, the basic essence had remained intact, and slowly, people began to change their world. In an effort to weed out the falsehoods, they began to search for clarity and wisdom.

An Overview of Our Situation

God's essence is LOVE. That love is self-aware, innate intelligence, energy, light, matter, desire, creativity, stillness and movement. It is All-Knowing. Love created all things, sustains all things, and permeates all things; there is *nothing* that is *not* God. God is everything. The most accurate and powerful name of God is I AM.

God, the Great I AM, begat his children, which were individual aspects of Himself. These children are known as the First Born. They exist in Thought and creative energy. The First Born, the I AM Children, eventually begat aspects of themselves in the form of Twin Rays of Light. These Twin Rays of Light have all the qualities of their parents. In addition, because of the laws of light, they took on a dual quality. One Ray was predominantly female, resting and reflective, and the other male, movement and creative.

These Twin Rays set out to explore and create in the realms of light. Many projected their consciousness into the densest forms of matter. After a time, they became attached to the sensations of physical identity. On Earth, these Separatists are known as the Dark Brotherhood.

The Twin Rays that settled this planet created many beautiful things in nature; forest, flowers, animals, and lived in perfect harmony with the environment. Immortal and telepathic, they created all they desired instantly from their thoughts using the light that was all around them.

Their physical bodies were less dense than the Separatist bodies, so they could easily dissolve their bodies when no longer needed. Sexual reproduction did not exist. The Twin Rays of Light communed with, and were directly connected to their Creator, the I AM Children.

The Dark Brotherhood convinced some of the Twin Rays to try out the dense physical bodies they had created. They told them about the wonderful feelings and sensations they would discover including a new sense of individual power. This intrigued some of the Twin Rays, and they took on the limited physical forms. Soon the physical senses became more dominant than the spiritual ones. And these Rays lost their freedom and power. Many religions talk about the fall of man, such as the Adam and Eve story.

In our world today, many of the stories of extraterrestrials and gods that exist are stories of the Dark Brotherhood, who created advanced technology in order to travel the universe and colonize planets. Now many of the religions of Earth mistakenly worship the Dark Brotherhood as the one true God.

The religious beliefs of the Dark instill fear. They generate a sense of helplessness, isolation, superiority, victim status, martyrdom and unworthiness. They promote a fear of judgment and promise eternal punishment (hell) if their beliefs are not obeyed.

In contrast, the teachings from the Counsels of Light impart a philosophy of love, peace, forgiveness, freedom, personal responsibility and empowerment. They teach that everything is connected, and that we are all made from the same essence, which is the Great I AM. The world of form and senses is not our true nature; it is only an illusionary shell. We have the ability to free ourselves from this illusion anytime we want. The only thing keeping us in our situation is our strong desire for, and attachment to, physical sensations.

We create our own reality. This law simply means that we get back in life what we give out; or, we will reap as we have sown. Because we have the power of creation within us, all that we think, feel and focus upon becomes our reality.

How we live today determines what will manifest tomorrow. The future is created by the thoughts and actions that we have and do today. For example, if we focus on the past, we bring that past into the present, which then creates the future. We are the only ones responsible for what we are experiencing. If we do not like the current situation, we are the only ones who can change it. We are the Creator in physical form, expressing ourselves in the worlds of matter. The only way to change the situation for the better is to face everything and avoid nothing.

If we desire freedom from the physical body or freedom *in* the physical body, we *must* take control of our physical senses and not let them rule us. We must be the master and not the other way around. We have Divine powers within us that have been forgotten and are dormant. They must be allowed the space to blossom and grow. This will never happen as long as we are slaves to our senses. We will never have true peace, happiness and abundance, as long as we are addicted to physical stimuli.

The Dark Brotherhood will use every trick they can to keep us ensnared. This is how they remain empowered. They feed off our energy and desires. They are no longer capable of generating light, because light is love and freedom, and they have separated themselves from that. We must want freedom and mastery over the physical world more than we want to indulge in it.

We have spent thousands of lifetimes in self-indulgent, self-centered, emotional behavior. We have spent thousands of lifetimes exploring our own personal dramas. What we are experiencing today is not unique; everyone has felt pain, abandonment, sorrow, torture, illness, addictions and betrayal. We need to get over ourselves.

There *is* a way out, but first we have to face up to our condition, take responsibility for it, and through strength and courage, begin to change it. For some this will take extraordinary effort. Others who have disciplined themselves along the way will find that reactivating their powers is easier. In trying to exert this kind of control over our senses, throughout history, we have swung from one extreme to the other. Following the path of poverty and abstinence, we have flogged, starved, beaten, isolated and purged just about everything we could from our bodies.

This way has been long and hard, but valuable. In today's world, we are now living in a self-centered generation that is extremely indulgent. We are guided by the philosophy that most behavior is okay because there is no right or wrong, just shades of gray, and it's all in how we look at it. We have taken a portion of the truth and used it to give ourselves permission to indulge in everything. This, too, has provided a valuable lesson. Each path has shown that neither path has brought the freedom and happiness we seek. These paths have served as stepping-stones to a greater understanding that what we are seeking we haven't yet found.

In each of our lifetimes, we recreate the past with slow growth and no real understanding of our problem. Our consciousness is trapped here on this physical plane of reality, and in between each lifetime, we do not leave, but stay attached to the physical world in a spirit body.

As disembodied Rays or Souls, we exist in a reality some have called "Purgatory" or the "Astral." This realm is full of the same sensory stimuli we had when we were in physical forms. We spend our disembodied time enjoying whatever form of sensory pain or pleasure we were attached to on Earth.

Those who spent their lives full of hatred, anger, meanness and violence experience these same offenses while they are disembodied after death. Others, whose lives were spent being kind and caring, have the same experiences while disembodied. People call this Heaven and Hell, but the truth is—we create our own reality whether in physical or spiritual forms. Then at some point, when the desire to re-embody becomes strong, we search for a family whose reality matches our own—and do it all over again. There is only one way to break the cycle of re-embodiment or reincarnation, and that is through a transfiguration of the physical body.

Part Two

Part Two reveals Jesus' true mission. A clarification is given about the Golden Age and the Second Coming. The Book of Revelations is reexamined and the nature of prophecy is discussed.

Jesus' True Mission

Throughout history, the lives of great people have been well documented. Why then has so much of Jesus' life been left out of history? For such an important man, there is scant detail about his life. One story here or there concerning his childhood, and then he simply vanishes until he is in his 30s. A lad with such wisdom who was teaching scholars in the temples would surely have been closely watched and documented.

The truth is that a great deal of Jesus' life has been suppressed or rewritten in order to satisfy the people in power. In order to keep the masses subdued and not incite rebellion, those in power created a religion around Jesus. With the threat of punishment and promise of rewards, they psychologically controlled the people.

The beauty of Jesus is that he offered humanity *a living example of what they used to be and could be again*. His very life was a demonstration of the power of the Rays of Light in full operation within the physical worlds. His mission was *to make a public demonstration of these abilities in order to create a permanent record of the potential of every person.*

Jesus was part of a new experiment, one designed by the I AM Children. This experiment would allow those who were trapped in corrupted bodies a way to release those bodies. As a Ray of Light uncorrupted, Jesus was sent by his I AM Father to achieve this purpose. In John Chapter 10, Jesus says, *"Is it not written in your law, 'I said, you are gods'? If He calls them gods, to whom the word of God came (and scripture cannot be set aside) can you say that the one whom the Father has sent into the world blasphemes because I said, 'I am the son of God?"*

There have always been Rays who disciplined themselves enough to allow their spiritual powers to manifest, such as great Indian yogis and Christian saints. People who were often recipients and witnesses to these powers documented them in writings and teachings. Most of these saints and yogis, however, had to spend a lot of their time in isolation away from the corruption of the world in order to achieve these abilities. Some went to isolated retreats where Immortals and uncorrupted Rays of Light lived. There they were offered education and assistance by the Immortals.

Jesus had a great deal of Immortal assistance. He traveled to India and Egypt spending time in their retreats. When he was ready, he returned home and began to demonstrate what was possible when you master the physical world and allow your Divine powers to manifest. As master of both his mind and body, this allowed his Creator, one of the I AM Children, to blend its consciousness with him and become *One*. Jesus often said, *"I and the Father are one."*

Jesus' new experiment would use the full power of his Father, the I AM, to break the blueprint of the Separatist form. This was accomplished in the ascension of Jesus. When Jesus spoke, *"I AM the Resurrection and the Life, whoever believes in me, even if he dies will live, and everyone who lives and believes will never die."* (John 11:25-26), he meant this literally. Speaking as the I AM consciousness to the people of Earth, Jesus was saying; if you believe in me and what I am demonstrating and follow this path, you too, will be able to do what I have done.

Jesus knew that by going public with his demonstrations and teachings, he would incur the wrath of the Separatists. Already immortalizing, he could have walked away without going through death and made his ascension in the Immortal retreats. Instead, he went though the public pain and torture to demonstrate for history what was possible for humanity.

After his crucifixion, when Jesus was placed in the tomb, he healed and restored his body with the assistance of the Immortals. Evidence of this can be found in the Gospel of Peter which recounts the events during and after Jesus' crucifixion. This Gospel was discovered in a monk's grave by a French archaeologist in 1886. Taken from *The Compete Gospels* is Peter, Chapters 9-11 and 13

"Early at first light on the Sabbath, a crowd came from Jerusalem and the surrounding countryside to see the sealed tomb. But during the night before the Lord's day dawned, while the soldiers were on guard, two by two during each watch, a loud noise came from the sky, and they saw two men come down in a burst of light and approach the tomb. The stone that had been pushed against the entrance began to roll by itself and moved away to one side; then

the tomb opened up, and both men went inside.

"Now when these soldiers saw this, they roused the centurion from his sleep, along with the elders who were also there keeping watch. While they were explaining what they had seen, they saw three men leaving the tomb; two supporting the third and a cross was following them. The heads of the two reached up to the sky, while the head of the third, whom they led by the hand, reached beyond the sky, and they heard a voice say, 'Have you preached to those who sleep?', and the answer was heard from the cross: 'Yes!' These men then consulted one another about going to Pilate. While they were still thinking about it, the sky appeared to open and another human being came down and entered the tomb.

"When the centurion's company saw this, they rushed out into the night to Pilate. As they were recounting everything they had seen, they became deeply disturbed and cried, 'Truly he was a son of god!'"

"And they [Mary Magdala and friends] went and found the tomb open and went up to it and saw a young man sitting there in the midst of the

tomb; he was handsome and wore a splendid robe. He said to them, 'Why have you come? Who are you looking for? Surely not the one who was crucified, he is risen and gone."

His ascension, however, was an entirely different event. Being immortal, one is still in the body one was born into, but now it is perfect in every way. The Ascension required the full anchoring of the I AM Father into the body of the Immortal Jesus in order to transform it. The blueprint of the Separatist body would be permanently destroyed as the full consciousness of the Father, the I AM, was anchored info Jesus.

Because the vibration of the I AM Children is beyond physical light and matter, it transformed the original body into a higher pattern-of-light body. The new ascended body was a blending of the Ray of Light and its parent; the I AM Children, in one body. The Dark Separatists had no way of controlling this new and improved light body blueprint. This new form allowed the I AM the creative ability to, through its Children, to separate itself and reunite itself in a new and more expanded way. The ascended body of Jesus now had all the knowledge of its Creator Father; the I AM Children, and all the experiences of the Rays of Light in separation. This remarkable event permanently anchored on Earth, a living visible blueprint for others to follow. Jesus' mission, as such, was not only to master the Separatist world, but to transform it. This new freedom would give the Rays of Light a brand-new existence beyond what was previously known. Even Immortals could benefit from this event.

The Separatists, however, realized they were witnessing the source of their demise, and thus, set about to isolate what Jesus had done as a one-time unique event. They twisted and distorted the truth in order to prevent others from following. This idea worked because people were easily convinced that immortality and ascension were impossible tasks, reserved only for a God-like Being—not humans. The Dark Brotherhood knew that too many people had witnessed the life of Jesus, so it hid, destroyed, and perverted many of the true teachings in order to give the masses a feeling of inferiority and helplessness. The Dark were so frightened of this new demonstration of ascension, that they gained control of the situation and created their own religion around Jesus. They kept this religion alive by instilling fear of eternal punishment and damnation.

Fortunately, the true teachings of Jesus survived in the many people who have ascended since then. These Masters formed a fellowship of Immortals and Ascended Beings who are continuously guiding and helping humanity. Jesus and these Immortal Beings are currently living in the Golden Age, which is promised to each of us who have the courage to follow his example.

There is No Second Coming

The Book of Revelations is one of the central documents that have caused so much confusion about a Second Coming. A new examination of this book needs to take place. According to Bible scholars, no one is even sure who wrote the book. The author calls himself John, but he could have been, in reality, an admirer or follower of John who wanted to give him the credit.

The Book of Revelations is full of fantastic creatures, horrific events and wild descriptions of a vision the writer had. Apocalyptic writings of this nature were quite popular from about 200 B.C. to 200 A.D. Many writers of that time used this type of symbolism and allegory to portray their teachings, and we need to read Revelations within the context of history. We have assumed incorrectly that the writer John was describing something in the distant future. From his limited point of view, John could only explain what he saw using the current understanding and terminology of the day.

Two thousand years later, we think we are the ones who understand Revelations—not the people of its time. In fact, the opposite is true. John did not write Revelations for people two thousand years into the future; no, he was writing to the Christians of *his time*. John described his visions in a language of symbolism, which he borrowed from the Old Testament prophets such as Ezekiel and Daniel. According to biblical scholars today, there were numerous apocalypse writings of this nature in *both* Jewish and Christian sects. The most fantastical and imaginative one happens to be included in the Bible.

Daniel's writings in the Old Testament were composed during a time of Jewish persecution. They were meant to guide and give courage to the Jews during a time of trial. Later, the Book of Daniel gained great popularity, because the same type of persecution was being inflicted by Rome on the Jews and the Christians. Daniel used these inspired visions to teach moral lessons and to help encourage the Jews to persevere in troubled times.

Jesus confirms this in Matthew, Chapter 24. He is discussing his return, tribulations and the end times when he says, *"I say to you, this generation will not pass away until all these things have taken place. Heaven and Earth will pass away, but my words will not pass away."* Jesus knew that his ascension would establish a new heaven or a new existence for humanity if they chose to follow him.

In all world religions, there have been prophets and teachers who have had visions. This is due either to the use of herbs (which alter their minds) or because of intense emotional trauma, near-death experiences, restricted physical movement (i.e. being confined in prison), or intense ecstatic devotion. People have used these mind-altering experiences to teach a particular belief and reassure the masses that the Heavenly Host had not abandoned them. While they interpreted their experience the best way they could, a mixture of fantasy, truth, and the awful reality of their time, in fact influenced them.

You see that there are many realms that the physical eyes cannot see. Some are filled with Beings of Light, while some are filled with Beings of Darkness. Inside these realms, wonderful and horrible things exist. When physical humans leave their bodies in a vision, out-of-body or ecstatic experience and travel there, they witness and experience reality *in that realm*. People living in those realms are not restricted by a physical body and can, therefore, shape-shift into all sorts of fantastical images.

Most people are inexperienced in traveling in the spiritual realms and therefore cannot sustain a fully objective analysis of what they are witnessing. Upon returning to the physical body, they can only interpret what they have seen with the knowledge and belief systems they have. What they write is totally subjective according to their own beliefs. The fact that people from every religion and every culture have had these visions tells one just how common it is, and how varied the results can be.

From what I have learned traveling in the astral/spiritual worlds, many of these events described in Revelations and other sacred texts are actually ones that have taken place in the astral kingdoms and not Earthly ones at all. Many of these spiritual realms are full of Dark kingdoms fighting great wars among themselves, while others are wonderful and full of highly advanced people who are spending their time between incarnations in spiritual bliss. Someone visiting these realms could witness events there, see the relevance, perhaps, to Earth, and write about it to inspire and educate. This is exactly what the writer John did. Having seen these wonderful places, he determined it must be the final reward for all the good souls on Earth, but he was only partially correct. Further explanation of this is in Part Four.

Why do you think fantasy, science fiction, witchcraft and the like are so popular among humanity? After death, or in between incarnations, we live in a world free from the restrictions of the physical body, and therefore, all kinds of Beings can exist and supposed magical events can take place. We retain these memory imprints when we reincarnate, and they naturally rise to the surface in books and movies, and a desire to return to those more free and magical days.

A Second Coming and Golden Age on Earth is not going to happen, as people believe from reading the Book of Revelations. In order to establish a new physical Heaven and new Earth with bodies that are immortal, you would have to have a complete shift for everyone simultaneously. The Dark Separatist reality we live in is a *false* belief or illusion, and the only thing holding it together is our addictions to it. In order to experience a Golden Age, you have to get everyone to let go of his or her reality.

The masses are hoping for an escape; they crave any prophet with a message of deliverance, any vision of Mary, any miracle, any sign of Extraterrestrials, all in an effort to make sense of their misery and be rescued. We have to free ourselves from our addictions before the ascended realms can aid us. Jesus said, "*The Kingdom of God is within you.*" The Jews of his time thought he was there to deliver them from Rome and set up a physical kingdom. People today believe Jesus will come again, defeat Satan, and set up a physical kingdom. However, Jesus has already set up a new kingdom in the higher vibrations of Light. The "Evil" or corrupted bodies have already been defeated, and the Golden Age is in progress; we just need the wisdom to understand Jesus' message.

Some people argue that they are seeing the fulfillment of prophecy in their times. They do not understand the universal law that states: *you create your own reality.* You have the power of the I AM within *you*, and what you desire, you create. Of course, there are also billions of other people on the planet all creating their own reality that has *nothing* to do with Revelations and Christianity. All these people are interacting and clashing with one another. So what kind of future could humanity possibly create for itself?

Jesus, the Immortals, and all the Rays of Light in the universe are not going to come here and, in one big battle, kill all the Dark Brotherhood and rescue the supposed Chosen Ones. We are *all* the Dark Brotherhood at one level or another. *We have to want to change our circumstances in order to live in a new one.*

Only when enough people on the planet are tired of playing the self-centered/self-indulgent game will we begin to see a new reality. Jesus lives in an ascended body which vibrates at a higher level of light than our own, and they are not compatible. When we have mastered the physical world and defeated death, we can live with him in the Golden Age he has already ushered in.

Jesus states this in his own words in the Gospel of Thomas. This original text was thought to be lost and was discovered among the Nag Hammadi Library in 1945. Thomas, Chapters 50-51 (from *The Compete Gospels*). Jesus said, *"If they say to you, 'Where have you come from?' say to them, 'We have come from the Light, from the place where the Light came into Being by itself, established itself, and appeared in their image.' If they say to you, 'Is it you?' say, 'We are its Children, and we are the chosen of the Living Father.' If they ask you, 'What is the evidence of your Father in you?' say to them, 'It is motion and rest.'*

"His disciples said to him, 'When will the rest for the dead take place, and when will the new world come?' Jesus said to them, 'What you are looking forward to has come, but you don't know it.'" Jesus reiterated this once again in Thomas 113: *"His disciples said to him, 'When will the Father's imperial rule come?' Jesus says, 'It will not come by watching for it. It will not be said, 'Look here or look there!' Rather, the Father's imperial rule is spread out upon the Earth, and people don't see it.'"*

Remember, our free will has placed us here. We wanted to explore and experience the physical world of sensations. We have spent thousands of lifetimes indulging in the senses; maybe now we are finally ready to move on beyond this reality. Many of us have, indeed, learned all there is to learn about the world and its experiences. After all, how many times can we eat; sleep; have sex; have children; fight; love; travel; work; experience pain, illness, sorrow and death before we have finally had enough? Never has the statement "been there, done that" been more true.

Part Three

Part Three presents the key things that one must do in order to achieve immortality. Every Immortal has understood and practiced these steps in order to achieve their victory. Advice is also given concerning the many spiritual and metaphysical paths one may study.

Our Intent

There is one law that you simply *must* understand, and it is this: Intent (motive) drives everything. It is the power in your life, and the key to your freedom. AS mentioned earlier, you create your own reality by what you think and feel. You have the power of God, the I AM, within you, and with that power comes responsibility. Your desire, motive and intent shape your reality and create your existence.

There are consequences to your actions. Most people are taught the old agricultural metaphor, *"You will reap as you have sown,"* yet they still act like out-of-control toddlers with no thought to the results of their actions. Jesus said that while the old law punished someone for committing murder, if you actually have hate in your heart, it is as if you have committed murder and the punishment will be the same.

Jesus understood universal law. He knew who he was—God, the I AM, in a physical body—and he knew the responsibility that carried. We are the same; everything we say, feel or do creates for good or ill. We simply must start living our lives in honesty and integrity, because any intention to deceive and lie will only bring pain. For example, one person can help another with genuine concern as their motive; in this case, he or she will reap a blessing from that action. Another person can do the same service, but if his or her intent is to gain financial reward for selfish reasons, he or she will reap a negative result. Selfish motives reap selfishness from others, which results in other people *using you* for *their* personal gain. This law is absolute, and the sooner people begin to operate *within* the law, instead of breaking the law, the better their lives will be. This may not be easy for those who have spent their lives releasing uncontrolled emotions on everyone with no regard for the results of their actions. However, if you want to improve your life and eventually gain freedom, you must begin to examine your motives and intentions for everything you do.

When you go to work, what is your motive? When you interact with different people, what is the motive? In doing something nice for your loved one, what do you hope to gain? If you ask people to elect you as a political representative, is it because you love the power and ability to manipulate others? When you vote to pass a bill in Congress, is your motive to improve people's lives or to gain a favor? Again, your intention creates your results. Perhaps you are a woman who has a lot of stress because you are taking care of children, a husband and your job. You believe you have to be "Super Mom" and do everything your family, parents and friends expect you to do. In your heart, however, you are building up resentment and feeling depressed and trapped. Subconsciously, you begin to fashion ways to escape your situation. Then you begin to consciously daydream about ways for people to feel sorry for you. You want permission to let go of so many responsibilities. Before you know it, you have created a disease such as cancer, multiple sclerosis or heart attacks.

Now suddenly, you are off the hook, and you have given yourself the permission you needed for going to the spa or taking a day of rest. Women have learned to play martyrdom rolls quite well. It would be healthier to just express your desire to reduce your stress and begin to improve the situation, regardless of what others might think. If you have done something for selfish reasons or to hurt another, you may think you have gotten away with it, but eventually the laws of cause and effect come back around. What you will then encounter is something ten times worse than what you gave out.

In the late 1990s and early 2000s, corporate high-level executives fulfilled their individual greed by stripping their companies of their wealth. In doing so, they brought about the wholesale destruction of their company. Ultimately, they lost not only their wealth, but also became criminals. What is true is that *there are no victims in life; everyone who suffers an event suffers because, at some point in their life, they created the very energy they are now suffering*. Eventually, even countries that seek to destroy and terrorize will reap their own destruction with equal or greater violence.

Remember that all actions are the result of *your* desires and intentions set into motion. You are a Creator. Perhaps you are not creating five thousand loaves of bread from one loaf now, but you are creating, nonetheless. You cannot escape the results of your actions. You cannot drink your troubles away on a Friday afternoon or pop Prozac (or the latest antidepressant pills) everyday and still hope to improve your situation. Numbing yourself only creates the same ineffectual results; you have to *change* what you do not want. You must take responsibility for your actions and the results of those actions. Face life head-on and become its master.

In addition, we are not responsible for other people's motives or feelings; they belong to them. For example, when someone decides to get angry with you for some action on your part, examine your motives in your heart. If you know your motives are innocent, then you are free. It is up to the other person to see why he is reacting and creating that feeling, not you. If you say something that hurts another, and they call you on it, stop and examine the reason why you did it. Taking responsibility involves examining your actions and motives.

If you had malice, anger, revenge, jealousy or hurtfulness behind your actions, the your must take responsibility for it. Apologize and make things right. It takes courage and moral fiber to hold yourself accountable for your actions. If you do not, however, the result will be someone else doing the same thing to you, only worse. We simply do not realize the power we have, and the more emotion we put into action, the stronger the results.

Have you ever noticed that when you pour all your energy into something, it is more successful than you could have ever imagined? That is because you are using your I AM powers of creation to *create*. The more energy you put into something, the bigger the result. The energy does not always have to be physical; there is a saying from *The Book of Runes*: *"More than Doers, we are Deciders."* Once the decision is made, the power of the I AM goes into action to produce the results, and the more certainty we have in our decision, the less physical effort is needed. In our original state as Rays of Light, before we became trapped, everything we desired with strong intent was manifested instantly in the physical. Jesus fed 5,000 people with only one loaf of bread and two fishes because he was master of his physical world. All that he desired manifested *without physical labor*.

Life was never meant to be a struggle; we just created it that way. All these thousands of years creating guilt, fear, lack and envy have produced a world of pain, struggle and death. Surely, we are tired of this game by now and desire to do something different. In order to have a new beginning, we must first eliminate self-centeredness.

Escaping Self-Centeredness

The first act of separation from our parents, the I AM Children, was self-centeredness. Immediately following this act was self-indulgence. Over time, we have made an art of self-study and self-absorption. Yet, for all the trouble our self-centeredness and self-indulgence has caused, we cannot judge this act as evil. We must remember that all things are the I AM expressing itself. Everyone and everything is God-in-action.

Our experiment in isolation or self-centeredness is only a game we play, an illusion we believe to be real. Many of us are now ready to take the knowledge we have gained from this experience and move on. Those who are not ready will just continue to play the game a little longer. Yet, all any teacher or teaching can do is point the way. They—or it—cannot save us; only we can do that.

Since we are all in this illusion together, we need to understand how to release ourselves from it. We must use our intent or desire to break the pattern of self-centeredness in order to regain our freedom. The first realization we must come to is that nothing we feel, think or do is unique; everyone has experienced the same thing at one time or another. In fact, we have had every experience a thousand or more times because of the many lifetimes we have lived.

In just one lifetime, we will experience the loss of—or betrayal by—a loved one, physical pain, mistreatment and fear. Equally, we will also experience incredible love, joy and wonderful days. These sensations are not new, nor are they unique *to you*; we are all experiencing the same illusion. *Getting over yourself and your own personal dramas is the first step.*

The next realization we must have is the understanding that in order to free ourselves from pain and sorrow, we must also free ourselves from pleasure and feel-good sensations. Both are addictions which keep us trapped. *There is no way to escape the pain without escaping the pleasures too.*

So when you go about your day, take your mind off yourself and your personal dramas, and expand your view to take in the whole. See things from a larger perspective. Realize that those whom you call your enemies suffer the same fears and pains that you do. They want love and security just as much as you do. *We are all the same, and my personal dramas are no different from yours, even if they appear so.* When you look at people around you, remember they are all going through the same thing, even if it does not manifest at that moment; it has in the past, or it will in the future.

I remember riding in a car house-hunting with a realtor once, and we were talking about some illness I had. When I was finished, she began to tell me how her husband had left for another woman. She had also survived a brain tumor and lost her brother to a brain tumor, all within the last six months. When we stopped to get gas and buy some water, the woman at the cash register was bald. She said she had just been going through chemotherapy, lost her well-paying job and was now struggling to make ends meet. *When you lose your self-centeredness, you develop compassion*. Compassion is an expression of love and another step towards freedom

It *will* take effort on your part to break your addictions and indulgences. Hollywood, the music industry and the media have caused a great deal of damage that keeps us enslaved to the senses. No matter what they try to tell you, what you expose yourself to and focus upon *does* influence your life. You are expending your life energy when you indulge in the senses.

You create your own reality, and if you focus on sexual or violent movies, music, reading material and the like, you are creating a bond with that sensation. That sensation will exert control over your life. It is the same with gambling, eating, drinking or drugs. *What you do with your life in this moment creates your future life.*

You cannot serve two masters; either you serve your I AM Presence within, or you serve your senses. The only way to be free from your senses is to break the attraction to the act you are doing. You must stop drinking, gambling or involving yourself in sexual indulgences. Even our desire for food must be broken. I once did a juice fast for thirty days, and right after that, I spent another three months fasting each week for four days and eating for three. That experience broke my need to eat for the sake of pleasure. What is required is disciplined motivation, and if you can get someone to do it with you, the process is much easier. Discipline builds character and strength, which you need in order to master any sense addiction.

I know many of you are saying: *how can I avoid the things of the world?* Some have done it by isolating themselves in caves and living away from the general population, but you can do it in your everyday life. Start by taking one thing that you think you cannot live without, and let go of it. It can be as simple as relinquishing coffee or alcohol. Keep your life on an even keel, and slowly begin to wean yourself off the things that control you. If you have to be at home to watch a certain television program, stop watching it altogether. The key is to *be the master of your world and not the other way around*. If there is some situation, object or sensation you cannot live without—that is the first place you need to start.

I am not talking about taking your insulin medication or anything else that you need for physical survival. I am talking about an *addiction* such as chocolate, sex, thrill-seeking, drinking and patterns that control you. Taste, touch, hearing, small, vision, sex, emotions: These are all creations of the Separatist body that keep you trapped by suppressing your spiritual senses and abilities.

We are addicted to more things than substances; you can also succumb to an environment or atmosphere. If you have to drink in order to feel good or socialize, a good test would be to go out on a Friday night after work with friends who want to drink beer and party. Can you order club soda and still have a good time with them? Perhaps you are invited to a dinner party of six, which is small enough for your actions to be noticed. When they start pouring the wine with dinner, can you say *"No, thank you"*? Overcoming your attachment involves not only abstaining, but also enjoying yourself while not craving the wine. If everyone at work is gossiping about someone, can you walk away and not be part of the desire to ridicule and judge? Do you perform acts of sex that you find distasteful just to be accepted and loved? *Every time you do something to "fit in" or be accepted, you become a slave to the world and not its master.* True mastery comes from the ability to say *"No"* to something and then not lusting after it in our hearts. It means not being stressed by having resisted the influence of peer pressure.

It may take many years to develop mastery over the senses, but the reward will be more love, peace, and in the end, freedom. When you truly eliminate attachment to desires, it frees your whole world, and new and wonderful things which had been dormant, can surface. I am not saying you cannot participate in life. As Jesus said, *"Be in the world, not of it."* There is a difference, and once you have mastered your cravings, attachments and desires, you can freely enjoy all things without the risk of them controlling you.

As much as medical science would like to pass off addiction as a fluke of your genetics, in reality, it is a result of spending hundreds, even thousands, of lifetimes indulging in a particular vice or sensation. Self-indulgent patterns are imbedded in our energetic memory. This energy remains with us from one lifetime to another, and without the proper discipline, we continue to indulge. People who own porn magazines, parade sex and lust on music-television and movies are people who have over-indulged in the sensation of sex, lifetime after lifetime. They are slaves to that lust.

The Dark Brotherhood feeds off the energy of lust and desire. They do everything they can to drag people under the spell of sensation. This is not hard for them to do because most people lack any real discipline and are easily led to their own demise. Since the Dark desires to keep these physical bodies, they will do everything possible to keep humanity from gaining their freedom. They feed on hatred, anger, power, greed and lust—the more intense, the better. This energy is what they use to keep reinforcing their reality, all the while suppressing your true nature, which is love and light.

Escape the spell of seduction, eschew self-absorption. Get your mind off you, your problems and your indulgences, and put your energy into constructive pursuits. Realize that most people around you are suffering with their own dramas and spend all their energy focused on themselves. When you add your dramas to their burdens, most people shut down or react selfishly, feeling overloaded. Try spending one week where you do not talk about yourself, your feelings and your problems. When you take the focus off you, you will be amazed at what you can do and how much better you will feel.

Navigating Spiritual Development

The road to mastery can seem like a long and hard one. It may even seem impossible. But remember your true nature—which is freedom, love and light—is stronger than any illusion, vice or sense addiction. Make the unwavering decision to take your focus off sensations and concentrate on love and spiritual development. Once you have done that and allowed a space for spirit to grow, it will blossom and begin to help change your life for the better. I was once explaining this to a man in California, and he said to me, *"But I love to eat, drink, smoke, gamble and have sex many times a day."* He said he loved the world and all its pleasures. My only response to him was, *"Then why are you so unhappy and miserable? What have you not gotten from the world that you are still looking for?"* You cannot force people to change, and you cannot go about preaching to them. They have to be ready. For some it will take more lifetimes, and that is perfectly fine since all is in Divine order.

We are all growing spiritually at our own rate. We have the right to do as we please because we are God, the I AM, to begin with. It is like the prodigal son who has left his father's home to go explore the world; once he had indulged in everything and still found only emptiness, he was ready to come home. All you can do is free yourself and, in the process, point the way for others. When they are ready, they will follow.

Fortunately, there are tools you can use to help accelerate the process. Many of these tools have been well explored; others are not as well known. A brief discussion of these tools follows.

Prayer and Meditation are the bedrock for all spiritual growth, but the reason most of our prayers and meditations are not very successful is the way in which we do it. Our prayers are usually begging God to help us in our hour of need. At other times, they are automatic recitals without reflection. Many even teach that we should meditate on nothingness, sitting quietly while we empty our minds. While this type of meditation helps to relieve stress and calm our emotions, it offers a much slower process to freedom.

Freedom and spiritual gifts comes from dynamic action and using your authority as a Child of the I AM, a Ray of Light. You must first claim who you are and then accept your Divine Birthright. No real change can happen until you let go of the idea that you are sinful, unworthy and made from—and will return to—the dust of the Earth. You are the Divine I AM in action, and you have the authority to create and produce whatever you desire. Start using that power to free yourself. Then speak your prayers from a sense of power and knowingness.

Whenever possible, say your prayers aloud in a commanding voice, and put all the feeling of power and authority you can behind your request. Because you have spent eons living in the shadow of helplessness, you will need to muster a large amount of conviction and authority to produce the results you want. You are trying to awaken the powers within you and gain the feeling of security that your actions *will* produce results. It is important to recognize that you should not approach prayer as a beggar going to the master's table for scraps. You are heir to all the riches of the Father and can request whatever you need in order to fulfill you purpose, *so long as your motives are pure*.

In the beginning you should pray for wisdom, love and determination. Pray to have your divine powers restored and for freedom from sense addictions. When you pray, realize you are calling upon your Creator, one of the I AM Children. Address him using the most powerful name of God you have: I AM. Say, *"Great I AM (or 'Mighty I AM,' or 'I AM Father') free me from this physical body and all its sense addictions. Restore all my divine powers and guide me to use them for my freedom and the freedom of others. Give me the wealth that is mine, restore my health, eliminate all avenues of seduction, and protect me with your armor of Light."*

Always remember, it is your right to have a healthy, bountiful and loving life. You were originally—and still are—perfect in every way. All things are possible to use and create. You are God in action; you are an expression of God "stepped down" from the realms of thought and desire into physical light.

As to meditation, two kinds of meditation can prove helpful to you. The one most people begin with is the stilling and quieting of the mind and body. This is normally done in the morning and evening for 20 minutes. There are hundreds of books on meditation, but essentially, what you are trying to do is gain control over the body and mind by forcing it to sit still and be quiet. When you are meditating, thoughts and feelings will come up, but the key is not to attach yourself to them. Let them pass and just keep focusing and relaxing and letting go. You can place your *intent* on allowing your spiritual nature to rise to the surface and to feel love within. Feel your body and emotions relaxing and filling up with well-being and peace. This type of meditation has a rejuvenating effect and clears the mind of clutter.

I begin each of my mediations with a relaxing and stilling session. Then I move into a more active meditation. In active meditations, you conceptualize and form pictures of what you want your life to be. You see your problems resolve. If you are ill, imagine yourself healed and perhaps doing an activity you enjoyed such as hiking or skiing. The idea is to absorb your mind and body into the image of health, become that health, and feel it in your body and emotions. Since you create your own reality, the more you create a positive reality, the sooner it will manifest.

The type of results you get will depend upon your ability to put all your feelings and desires into what you are trying to manifest. The stronger your feelings and desires are, the better the results will be. When you are finished with this type of active meditation, it is important to see the image as real and not doubt the results. Know that things are working in the universe to bring about what you want. You can also use an active verbal prayer-request at the end of your meditation to reinforce the new image you are creating.

Master the Physical and let go of addictions. You cannot be slovenly and lazy with your body; your body needs discipline. Out of habit, your body will crave all kinds of things which do not produce freedom, but instead, produce attachments. Keeping that in mind, you should begin to let go of the things that are the *most* obstructive to your freedom. The goal is to purify the body and mind of physical attachments, thereby enabling more of our true spiritual nature and divine powers to manifest. What Jesus did, each of us can do, and that includes so-called miracles and even defeating death.

Here are some suggestions that will help free you from attachments:

✠ **Food**. The process of eating things from the Earth is a Dark Force pattern of behavior. This pattern will only reinforce your attachment to the Earth. This does not mean you should stop eating tomorrow; what is means is that your true reality does not need anything of the Earth to live.

Always remember, you are a Being of Light, and Light is what you were created from and sustains your true nature. This is not a diet for health or doctor-prescribed longevity; this is a diet to enhance your spiritual nature. Many people eat all kinds of things and live to be in their 90s, while others eat very healthy diets and die young. This diet is designed to help free you of physical addictions and lessen the burden to your physical body, which will allow more of your spiritual powers to manifest.

Animals are one of the most important things on the list to eliminate. Because they have a consciousness, they go through birth, pain, suffering and death. These patterns are imprinted into their bodies, and when you eat an animal, these imprints reinforce pain, suffering and death in your consciousness. So start by eliminating mammals: cows, goats, sheep, dogs, cats, deer, elk, pigs and the like, eating only fowl and fish.

Eventually, let go of fowl and eat mostly saltwater and fresh fish. It is permissible to eat unfertilized eggs along with some dairy. However, the problem with dairy is that it is mucous-forming, allergenic and clogs the colon. As plenty of soy products have become more available to replace dairy, save your dairy for those occasions where only dairy will do. For example, use soymilk on your cereal and soy ice cream. Fish, eggs and dairy give plenty of protein. They are lighter in vibration and cellular memory than beef, pork and chicken.

Also, eliminate artificial sweeteners, artificial chemicals and preservatives. Many books document the harmful effects of sugar, caffeine and manufactured chemicals. So use as many organic or natural food products as you can. Choose natural sugars such as maple syrup, natural non-processed can juice, stevia (a root), and the like. In addition, reduce or eliminate caffeine; it is a drug and designed to enslave your nervous system.

✠ **Alcohol**. One should completely eliminate hard liquor. Alcohol is a poison; it has no value and does great harm. No matter what the medical community says about the value of drinking two or three glasses of wine everyday for your health, it is a lie spun by the Dark, designed to keep you enslaved to your senses. I suggest only an occasional glass of wine that is produced organically with little sulfites. Again, you must judge your own self-control.

✠ **Detox**. Keep your body clean! There are literally dozens of books on detoxifying, fasting and cleansing. Do some research and find what works best for you. Here are some things I have discovered over the years that work for me. First, I drink lots of water, but not just any water. I try to find bottled water that is high in pH (potential of Hydrogen) and no salt. The two I regularly use are Evamor and Essentia. Our bodies are too acid and this causes aging. Keep your body pH neutral to alkaline. If you are like me, it is almost impossible to do that through foods alone, so I use high pH water with a pH of at least 8-9 to keep me balanced.

Next, vacuum your skin, that's right—with a vacuum cleaner such as the Hoover Wind Tunnel. This is my best-kept secret. Most of us are familiar with exfoliating our skin in the shower; it is a good way to get rid of dead skin and stimulate blood flow. Vacuuming, however, goes way beyond that. Use the hand attachment on the Hoover, which is about one inch wide and four inches long with small teeth, and go over as much of your body as you can. I am not claiming any medical miracles, but here is what I have found. The strong suction, along with your upward "towards the heart" movements, really stimulates a lot of blood flow. It breaks loose all the stored toxins hiding just beneath the surface of your skin in fat cells. If you vacuum your underarm area, this detoxifies your lymph nodes. All these toxins are now circulating in the blood—ready to be eliminated. Drink plenty of water before and after one of these sessions to make sure they do not settle back into the body.

You might have some heart palpitations after one of these sessions, at least I do. I believe this is because the toxins, or poisons, which are circulating in the blood, stimulate the heart. It settles down after a while, but I highly recommend you talking to your doctor before vacuuming if you have any concerns. After doing this for a while, I found the greatest benefits are two of the things that most people want anyway. It helps to regulate your weight and diminishes cellulite. Other than mild heart palpitations, other experiences (or side effects) are a slight headache caused from the toxins and mild bruising, if you vacuum in one place too long.

The benefits far outweigh any discomfort. Regularly eliminating the toxins and poisons that have built up in your body has valuable health benefits, and it helps constipation, muscle aches and general soreness. Most importantly, by keeping your body clean, more spiritual energy such as the Sacred Fire (discussed in Part Four) can be anchored in your body. I would suggest vacuuming two or three times a week, depending on your tolerance. Of course, you need to detoxify your liver and colon from time to time as well. There are herbs that can help you do this, along with seasonal fasting for two to three days.

✠ **Sex**. Another myth propagated by those who are addicted to the senses, is the value of sex. Whole religions have been created around sex claiming that it leads to enlightenment; all sex ever leads to is death. Sex is one of the most deadly addictions we have. It was created as a way to produce more sense-oriented Dark Force bodies. The act of creating a new sense body is totally engulfed in one of the strongest sense addictions there is—the orgasm.

I want to make this perfectly clear so there is no doubt; the Dark Forces created and use sex as a toll to enslave and keep you from ever gaining your freedom and true identity. There is no value to sex; it only creates more sense bodies into which more enslaved Rays of Light can incarnate. If everyone stopped having sex tomorrow, the world would be a better place. We need to transform the planet, not produce more vehicles for our senses! Every time you have sex, you are using the Life-force for sensual pleasure, which creates addiction.

I realize this will be the hardest addiction to relinquish, but if you start to gain some self-control over your sex life, with time, you will increase the spiritual essence in your body and subdue the desire for sex. If you are in a situation with a partner who requires sex in order to have a happy home life, then at least strive for moderation and then only as an act of loving another and not just for sensual pleasure. Hollywood and liberal philosophies have been tools of the Dark who wish to keep your senses fully activated and your addictions alive. Avoid places such as Las Vegas, New Orleans, gambling casinos and anywhere where self-indulgence and extreme behaviors are glorified.

You might be wondering—*well, what can I do?* That all depends upon you. If you are young and immature and the desire to see and do everything is still strong in you, you are not ready to do anything *but* enjoy the world. If however, you have done all that and seen that it does not bring happiness, just temporary pleasure, then perhaps you are ready to change your life. The point is: will you be an addicted human or a freed one?

When you can honestly and joyfully abstain or walk away from any of the sense addictions and nothing owns or controls you, then that is the beginning to freedom. Once you have mastered that hurdle, you will be ready to develop more of your spiritual abilities such as telepathic communication with others; healing; teleporting your body from one place to another; creating things such as food, money and housing from pure thought; immortalizing your body and a host of other abilities.

Throughout history, there have been great saints and sages who have performed some of these abilities. Although they may have died or had some minor attachments, the power of their true self was stronger than the seductions of the world. When you let go of the world, what replaces it are things far greater. Some of the ecstatic experiences I have had far surpass any physical pleasure or sexual orgasm. Union with the Creator is an unbelievable pleasure that sends waves of joy beyond measure through every fiber of your being. You will never lose by giving up the world; you will only gain.

When you are no longer attached to the world, it actually allows you to enjoy the world in a freer way. You can still have a nice dinner, a glass of wine with friends, go hiking in the mountains, have a massage and share many different ways of intimacy with your lover. But your motives are entirely different. Intent is the key, and with attachment and addiction gone, you are able to feel and express more love.

Some people think that "letting go of the physical" means you should shun the world entirely by sitting in a room meditating and neglecting your physical body. This could not be farther from the truth; we are talking about *mastery* of the world, not running away from it. True mastery is being able to command the powers of nature and the forces of the elements to do what *you* desire. It means being an active and creative force in the world of physical light. When you do not have attachments dragging you down, you have more freedom and creativity to produce in the world. What you are striving for is mastery of yourself and environment.

This means keeping up your appearance: good hairstyles, good clothes, healthy body, good manners, versatile abilities and having grace and poise. It does *not* mean being obsessed with your appearance. It is one thing to do something occasionally to improve your appearance; it is quite another to be obsessed. I know a woman who owns a spa, and, literally, there is nothing on her that has not been altered. She has had three breast implants, liposuction, several face-lifts, nose reconstruction, a fanny lift, a tummy tuck, lip injections, Botox injections—and she is only 35 years old. This behavior reflects self-absorption and an addiction.

As a whole, our culture is too obsessed with physical appearance. I believe this comes from a deep-seated memory in our Soul of when we had beautiful, perfect bodies that did not age or die. However, we cannot regain that body using physical techniques. We can only achieve that body through regaining our spiritual identity.

There is a right way and a wrong way to do something *if* you are interested in mastery. If you are not interested, but want to indulge in the world of the senses, then of course, everything is permissible. The choice is yours. I have found that the more spiritual you are, the more conservative you become. I know that most liberal New Agers will be amazed by that thought, but it is the truth.

I am not talking about being conservative in terms of religious dogma or fear-based conservatism. As you grow spiritually, you naturally move from what feels like enforced rules as a child under parental control to expressing yourself more freely without limits. As you mature, you realize that the exploration into the senses did not bring the happiness you were seeking, and you begin a journey inward instead of outward. This process naturally brings a more conservative and wiser path. Your actions are tempered with accountability.

A Very Powerful Tool to Transform Your Life is *People*. When you get like-minded people together, all focused on accomplishing a goal, the power in that can move mountains. Enough cannot be said about this. *If you want to progress faster, get with others in a group,* *say your prayers aloud, meditate and work on improving your diet and personality*. Keep each other honest in a loving, safe environment and create dynamic group energy. If there are ten of you, the energy is ten times stronger than with one person, and each person in the group benefits from the power at ten times the strength.

It is also an important part of mastery not to be judgmental; remember we all have flaws. Offer your help and correction with skill and pure intentions, not judgment. Remember that intent and motive is *everything*. This is why you have not seen more demonstrations of miraculous powers and immortality. The momentum of thousands of years of the opposite energy of destructions, bondage and death has been very powerful. We now need to build a different momentum; we need to gather millions of people together and actively work on the path of immortality. Then it would become easier for each of us and more visible in the outer world.

Dreams and Out-of-Body Experiences are a valuable resource for spiritual growth. Dreams are a mixture of working out problems, guidance and premonitions. In our dreams, we often interact with our loved ones and others who are dreaming. Occasionally, we interact with Rays of Light who were never in an Earthly body who have transcended them.

These beings are called Guardian Angels or Spirit Guides, and they impart information to us in the dream world. The more conscious you are in the dream world, the faster you can grow spiritually. Try to remember your dreams and write them down, but more importantly, do everything you can to become more *awake and aware* in your dreams. If you can be conscious, this opens a completely new world for you.

I have been a conscious dreamer and out-of-body traveler all my life and the amount of wisdom you gain is great. You can talk one-on-one with the Immortals, Jesus and advanced Beings, thereby gaining great insight and truths. One thing you need to understand about our-of-body travel us that you are taking your spiritual body out of the physical body and traveling in a slightly less physical realm. This realm, sometimes known as the Astral/Purgatory realm, is full of people just like you, and of course, full of the Dark Forces. Most of them are not going to have any more wisdom than you do.

The Dark Forces can disguise themselves as friends, relatives and other appealing people to try and influence you. Just because you are in a different reality does not mean that the Universal Laws are suspended; you will reap as you have sown in this realm as well. Therefore, if you are using self-control during the day, but at night, in your dream world you are having sexual orgies, gluttonous binge eating or drunken parties, you are binding yourself even tighter to the physical world. You are subjecting your spiritual body to the sensations of the physical world, thereby creating even heavier chains around yourself. This is why it is imperative that you become conscious in your dream world, so that you can start to control your experiences there and begin to master them.

Conscious dreaming is the same as out-of-body travel, only usually you do not have the sensation of leaving your body; instead, you simply "wake up" in another reality. Once you can say to yourself, "*I am dreaming,*" that is the moment you begin to take control over what you are experiencing. If it is destructive, you can stop it immediately. You may have had only an instant of recognition, but it is a beginning.

Here is an example of what you are trying to do. Your consciousness is like the size of an orange. You are very comfortable with the size and shape of that orange, but when you take that consciousness into the dreaming plane or astral plane, something happens. The spirit world is the size of a grapefruit, larger and more expanded. When your smaller consciousness (the orange) goes into the world of the grapefruit, it cannot fathom or hold onto that new reality. The result is you lose control and fall back into your old comfortable orange-sized reality. The key is to keep trying—keep working at being aware in this new reality. Eventually, you will be able to stabilize your consciousness in the grapefruit-sized world and function there normally.

Once you gain control over your dream world, you can project your spiritual/astral body anywhere you want. I routinely sit in on counsel meetings concerning the plans for Earth and, particularly, the United States, which is playing a key role. These abilities allow you to become an active participant, even though you are still tied to the physical.

It is in our dreams where people sometimes make contact with what we call Extraterrestrials or Aliens. Some well-known aliens called the "Grays" are actually Rays of Light from other planets who became trapped in their own physical bodies and are now visiting and meddling in our world. They chose the method of cloning versus sexual reproduction, but they are still addicted to their own reality. Many of them destroyed their worlds and are now using ours as a place to colonize.

I have encountered these Beings and others in both the astral and physical realms. They tend to abduct people by paralyzing their physical and spiritual bodies. Most abductees who are able to recall what happened to them often consider the experience to be a dream and not reality. The experience, however, is very real, no matter what reality it is.

Extraterrestrial Contact. I once rescued a person from abduction by these aliens known as the Grays. These aliens are the bigheaded, large-eyed beings with small gray bodies that many have encountered. This person does not wish to have his or her identity revealed, so I am referring to him or her as "my friend." One weekend, after buying crystals in Arkansas, we decided to stay in a cabin located in a remote wooden area. The cabin had one small bedroom with an old double-sized bed which we shared. That night after we went to bed, while I was traveling out-of-body, someone came up to me and told me my friend was in trouble, and I should get back to my body. When I returned, the Grays had just begun their abduction of my friend.

As the aliens were beginning to levitate my friend's body off the bed, I grabbed onto it, and some sort of energy beam lifted us through the ceiling. I began communicating telepathically with the Grays, and suddenly we stopped, hovering in midair just above the treetops. The ship was kicking up a strong wind and the trees were blowing and bending, but we remained suspended in their energy beam.

I called upon some extraterrestrial friends whom I knew were patrolling the area, and two of their ships showed up. One ship engaged the Gray ship, and the other ship intercepted our energy beam using its own energy beam. It then lowered us back through the ceiling and onto the bed. My friend who was being abducted did not have the ability to travel out-of-body or be conscious in the dream world. Not having this ability made it easy for the aliens to paralyze his or her bodies.

At another time, I lived for a short while in a cabin on a large hill in Southern Colorado. Beside my home on this hill was another house where several dogs lived. One night, I awoke from sleeping because I felt someone was in the room, and there, at the foot of the bed, were standing two Venusians and their android. The Venusians were about seven feet tall and wearing robes with belts tied around their waists. Their heads were much longer than ours, and they had very long slender fingers. They told me they had a base underneath my hill and needed to turn on some equipment for a while. They said the equipment might interfere with my energy fields and wanted to know if they could insert a device in my neck that would protect me from the interference. The device, they said, would be removed later, so I agreed.

One of the Venusians came over and placed a small object into the back of my neck. About 30 minutes after they had left, the ground and house began to vibrate. It wasn't severe tremors like those in an earthquake; it was a rapid, gentle vibration.

The next day I ran into my neighbor, and he was very perturbed. He asked me if I had felt the hill moving last night. He said his dogs barked the whole night, and the hill felt like it was vibrating. I just said, *"How interesting."* Three days later the Venusians removed the object and I never heard from them again. It is important to know that if you are ever visited by Rays of Light (extraterrestrials) from other planets, they will never instill fear. They will always seek your permission and cooperation with whatever they are doing. *Only Separatist extraterrestrials will do something against your will.*

Concerning Psychics and Channelers. I recommend that you do not use these avenues. Psychics are tapping into the astral world where disembodied spirits live, and they are getting information from them. Occasionally, they can even connect with Dark Forces disguising themselves. When they do contact a well-meaning spirit, the spirit usually does not have any more insight than you do and are often wrong in their judgments. Regarding Channelers. I channel, and I am sensitive to energies. It is very rare that you are actually working with Rays of Light who are not trapped in the physical worlds, but are actually in the higher realms of light.

If you want to receive guidance for problems, I suggest that you buy a deck of Angel or Tarot cards, or the Runes, and learn to use them yourself. No one knows more accurately what is right for you than your own I AM Self. Sit down and, in a direct prayer addressing your Glorious I AM, request guidance concerning the problem and do a reading.

I Do Not Advise Engaging in Magic. Working with the Powers of Nature and the Forces of the Elements only binds you to them, and they are part of the physical. I have spent a lot of time studying hermetics, alchemy and magic, and I can tell you that there are very few people involved in these arts who have ever gained their freedom from the physical world. The only one you can find in public records is the alchemist Comte de Saint Germain, whom I will discuss later. I have a few Elementals (nature spirits) that live with me; Poppynotch, Penelope and Bartholomew, but they have a specific purpose and come from the Sacred Fire.

Once you have mastered the physical world, you can command the elements like Jesus and Saint Germain did, but one must remember: *they had completely detached themselves from physical addictions before commanding the elements.* Most of the magicians throughout history and today are very addicted to the physical world and use the Powers of Nature to increase their physical pleasures and wealth. Always remember that the Powers of Nature and Elemental kingdoms are not evil; they are conscious entities of Light, which the Creators created in order to assist in the formation of the physical worlds. Rays of Light also used these beings and manifested more of them when creating the animal and plant kingdoms here on Earth. However, the Powers and Elementals can be dominated and controlled by the Dark to do horrendous things, and this is called "Black Magic."

Dark Forces and/or Brotherhood. First we have to remember that in the broad sense of the word, we are *all* the Dark Brotherhood: fallen, trapped and addicted to sensation. It is a common belief among New Agers to consider themselves as special Lightworkers. They believe they are here visiting from other planets in order to help the poor lost souls on Earth. The truth is if you were born in a physical body, and you are not yet immortal, you are just as much of the problem as everyone else. In fact, some of the most self-indulgent people I know are New Agers! The New Age movement spends most of its time fascinated with their own personal dramas.

The various levels of spiritual awareness among humanity are, in reality, just varying degrees of Light and Dark. We live among all kinds, with most of us being a mixture of both. Most people are not aware of the *really Dark Ones* that influence us. The Dark Forces' goal is to keep people enslaved to their senses and emotions. This is how they stay in power. By enslaving the whole world, they have a regular feeding ground to vampire energy. There are lesser Dark Forces, called Minions, who do the bidding of the ones in power, and these are attached to you as soon as you are born. They follow you from lifetime to lifetime, becoming so intertwined that you do not know your own emotions from theirs. They act like parasites, attaching themselves to your energy fields (mostly in the spinal column and nervous system). Their job is to keep your emotions stimulated, so they can feed on the energy you release. The bigger piranha-like Dark Forces then feed off them. Most people are just food sources for the Dark Forces, never really aware of the more powerful ones, except occasionally in the dream worlds.

However, if you start to awaken and take control of your life, then it becomes another story. The more dangerous ones then start to work against your progress and, with time and persistence, create scenarios to distract you from getting too far in your mastery. They often do this through finances and sex. For example, if they can keep you busy trying to survive making ends meet, you won't have much time for spiritual awakening. The other tool they use, which has become the addiction of choice, is sex. They have so mastered this sensation that virtually everyone is addicted! Psychological and educational training has been created to convince us that sex is a part of nature, and we need it in order to be balanced and well-adjusted. Condoms are given out in schools and Viagra is prescribed for adult men. Now, because our culture says sexual gratification is so important, elementary and junior-high school children are daily engaging in oral sex parties! Is there anything more sub-human and disgusting than putting your mouth where someone else urinates and defecates?

In fact, in terms of addictions, oral sex and masturbation have been some of the Dark Brotherhood's biggest triumphs. After all, what

the Dark wants is a person to be self-indulgent over and over again. Every time you orgasm, you release powerful energy upon which they feed. Next to an all-out war or violence, this is their food of choice. Lust has permeated our religious institutions, schools and political institutions—right up to the highest office. Sex is all over the movies, music and social scene. The sexual act devoid of love is pure lust, which is what the Dark Brotherhood craves the most.
I have had many encounters with the Dark Forces, and on occasion, they were so mad at me that they have scratched, bruised and even thrown me across the room. Some of this behavior arises from the fact that I have spent time in the astral plane—rescuing people from them, and this has upset them greatly.

I remember one particular encounter that happened after I had experienced a state of rapture. One afternoon, I came home from the store with my new Thomas Kinkade calendar and sat down on the living room floor scanning through his paintings of wonderful mountains and garden scenes. I came across a particular painting of a beautiful garden with a stairway that seemed to lead straight into heaven. My eyes followed the stairs upward into a ray of sunlight that beamed down from the sky, and I was immediately pulled from my body and soared into the heavens! Waves of ecstasy came over me, as uncontrollable tears poured down my face. I was in and out of consciousness for sometime before I finally came back into my body. It was a beautiful experience.

However, that night was very different. After retiring to bed, a very nasty Dark Force showed up. He looked pure demonic with claws on both his hands and feet. The room turned icy cold as he tore the blanket from my body. I was resting on my stomach, and he pounced upon my back and pinned me down to the bed. He snarled, howled, and cursed horrible things to me. He told me I would not be permitted to fulfill my destiny and began to try and alter the nervous system in my spine.

I fought him off and turned around, as he scratched and clawed my body. I was able to release the Sacred Fire from my hands, which pushed him back. However, he was able to grab me, and he threw me against the wall. I began calling for help, and more of the Sacred Fire built up around me like a pillar of Light. Realizing he could not penetrate this force field without being consumed, he just stood there cussing at me and finally left. So be forewarned: *The more light you have and use, the more you will incur their wrath.* They do not want even one person gaining their power and then leading others to do the same. Their human form can also cause trouble.

One cold winter evening, I was giving a talk at a restaurant that was open for breakfast and lunch and, in the evenings, sponsored lectures on interesting topics. While driving to the meeting, a car cut in front of me rather aggressively. I noticed the license plate read "EVIL," and I immediately saw this as a warning.

Later at the restaurant, about 20 minutes into my lecture, a woman arrived dressed in a full-length mink coat. She made a noisy entrance and climbed through several people to sit in the front row. Shortly after she sat down, the lights in the room began to flicker and then went completely out. Everyone was sitting in the dark and we could hear a strange hissing sound. I asked the restaurant manager if she had any candles and, fortunately, she did. We gathered the dinner tables into the center of the room and placed the candles on the tables. We continued the lecture, and this infuriated the woman in the dark mink coat. She got up, knocking chairs over as she left the building.

I have had plenty of run-ins and physical fights with them, and I can tell you from my own personal experience that, over time, your ability to deal with them gets better. There is a certain point in your own spiritual development when you have eliminated enough fear that the Dark Forces simply become a nuisance, at best. Of course, some of it depends upon your purpose, but for years now, I no longer see them as a threat when they try to interfere. Some of them are even asking to be led into the Light. However, they never give up, and you will never be free from them until you have made your ascension, as Jesus did.

The most important thing to remember is that nothing is more powerful in the universe than love. These Dark Force souls are our brothers and sisters who are more deeply rooted in fear and addictions than most of us. Once they respect you, you can use your power of love to help them, and there is nothing more rewarding. Even though this illusion of separation seems wrong, it is, after all, a learning experience and in perfect Divine Order. Some may take a little longer to get there, but eventually, even the most addicted soul will welcome freedom.

TOFU TURKEY POEM

TOFU TURKEY IS REALLY NEAT

TOFU TURKEY IS FUN TO EAT

TOFU TURKEY DOESN'T HAVE ANY FEATHERS

cause TOFU TURKEY IS PRESSED TOGETHER

TOFU TURKEY WON'T MAKE YOU CRY

cause no TURKEY HAD TO DIE

TOFU TURKEY IS MADE OF BEANS

TOFU TURKEY IS POLITICALLY GREEN

put TOFU TURKEY ON YOUR PLATE

this THANKSGIVING—

I CAN HARDLY WAIT!

Part Four

Part Four introduces the Sacred Fire to the reader; its purpose, history, and use. This section also discusses the difference between a resurrection and an ascension, as well as the difference between Immortals and Ascended Masters. America's true purpose in the world is presented. A "centered" approach to our religious and political differences is also offered.

The Sacred Fire

The Sacred Fire is a gift from our I AM Parent to us. It is a powerful source of energy, which originated at the source of all life in our universe. This seat of power is known as the Great Central Sun. The Great Central Sun is the "Eye" of the I AM for our universe. This central energy point, or Eye, connects with all the other central energy points in all the other universes. In this location, many of the I AM Children dwell and commune with their Father, the Great I AM. The Sacred Fire is the fire of creation. This Fire can destroy and rebuild all thought energy patterns in the universe. In a way, it "overrides" previous creations or programs.

Our parents, the I AM Children, qualified this Fire to override or annihilate the Separatist blueprint and their creations in physical form. When activated by us, a "descension" of this Fire occurs. It is released from our Creator and goes directly into our Being. This Fire was the flames of Pentecost, which gave the disciples their power. This energy is incorruptible; nothing can alter its essence. Jesus used this Fire to make his ascension into a new incorruptible body capable of existing in both the I AM Children's worlds and the physical worlds of Light. This Fire contains, within it, many unique qualities. Some of these qualities are purification and dissolving, realignment and restoration, creation and manifestation, and transfiguration. The Fire can eliminate our attachments to physical sensations and restore our powers.

Mystics have often referred to this Fire as the "fire that purifies the soul." Some who have experienced the Sacred Fire in ecstatic states talk about the intensity of love they feel; it is more than they can bear and consumes all that is not pure. The Fire's qualities can manifest in the body in different ways. When active, it may not be noticeable at all, or there may be a sense of motion like waves, pulses, spinning or other sensations. Depending upon how purified your body is, and how well you have let go of addictions, determines some of the Fire's capabilities within you. Once established in the body, it acts as a protective force-field repelling or consuming all that is not like it- self. Yogis have taught others about a fire that enlightens the mind and, for some, restores their powers. Western mystics have used a portion of this Fire known as the Violet Flame to purify and consume all human discord and imperfections. What is certain; however, is that anyone who has regained his or her powers and/or defeated death used the Sacred Fire in some form.

I have been consciously using the Sacred Fire for about nineteen years now. Because I also used the Fire in other lifetimes, I was born in this lifetime with some of my abilities already intact. These abilities are: conscious dreaming, out-of-body travel, sensitivity to energies, the ability to communicate with other realms of light, occasional precognition, teaching, and healing. These spiritual abilities act as the foundation for my current work with the Fire. A great deal of my sleep time is spent rescuing people in the Purgatory/Astral realms from the Dark Forces. I have also helped people in the physical world with demon possession and healings of various kinds, sometimes known or unknown to the recipient. I can absolutely say without question that the Sacred Fire works and can do amazing things in accordance with your purpose and development.

One such example was when I used the Sacred Fire for healing, a number of years ago. One of my friends had been going through many bouts with cancer and subsequent long hospital stays. During one of these episodes, he had been in the hospital for several weeks going through chemotherapy treatments. A decision was made to operate, and after surgery, he did not regain consciousness. The doctors feared he would lapse into a coma. The night I was visiting, the doctors had decided that in the morning they would do a spinal tap to see what could be causing the problem.

While I was there, the family's pastor came to visit. My friend's wife and I were sitting in the room when he arrived. He called her out into the hallway so they could talk. Things were looking very bleak, and I saw the distress and tears in her eyes as he tried to comfort her. The whole situation began to bother me, and I went over to my friend's bedside and held his hand. While he lay there unconscious, I placed my other hand upon his heart, and in a soft but very determined voice, I said aloud, *"Do something!"* I was speaking to my I AM Presence, and next I said, "*Come on Fire—activate!*" Within seconds of invoking these actions, the Sacred Fire was activated and poured through my whole body. I held onto him until the Fire subsided.

Afterward, I walked outside and said goodbye to my friend's wife and their Pastor. I really had no expectations of anything. I reasoned in my mind that the energy he received was spiritual and would probably help him spiritually.

After I went to bed that night, in an out-of-body experience, both my friend and his wife came to visit me. He told me that he had given up and was tired of struggling, until I had helped him. He said the energy I had given him cleared his mind, and he realized that he wanted to live. He said that he had regained consciousness and would make a full recovery. Both he and his wife thanked me and told me how grateful they were for my help. The next morning, I called the hospital to see how he was doing. His wife said, "*It was amazing, right after you left, he woke up and asked for some ice cream.*

They are letting him go home tomorrow!"

I was overwhelmed with joy because, not only was my friend well, but I had also proved to myself, once and for all, the power of the Sacred Fire to heal. I never told them what I did or that they had visited me in the spirit world. What was more important to me was that this experience was a turning point. It gave me confidence that the Sacred Fire really works for healing.

Another gift the Sacred Fire brings is the added power of the I AM to your own will and commitment. This added power helps you eliminate addictions much faster, break through patterns easier, and accelerate your growth at speeds that would normally take a hundred more lifetimes to accomplish. If everyone on the planet used the Sacred Fire daily in meditation, we could transform this planet in one generation.

How to Activate the Sacred Fire. Mystics throughout history have written about the Fire. Saints have accomplished this activation through ecstatic prayer, and yogis have taught various breathing techniques. Most of the techniques have not been very successful for many of their followers, because the followers did not understand that they must release their attachments to the physical, as well as to death itself.

In the 1930s, Godfre Ray King wrote several books that described the use of a portion of the Sacred Fire known as the Violet Flame. This flame is used for purifying and eliminating all human imperfections. This was a great leap forward in our ability to set ourselves free from the world of addictions. I suggest that anyone who is interested in pursuing immortality read his books, *Unveiled Mysteries* and *The Magic Presence*. He gives a full description of how to use the Violet Flame as was related to him by the great Immortal and Ascended Master, Saint Germain. To activate the Sacred Fire, you need to make a direct appeal to the I AM Father. Choose a time when you can spend as much time as needed in prayer and meditation. Make this activation a ceremonial event where you bathe, put on clean clothes and, in a quiet space, focus all your thoughts and determination upon activating this most holy Fire. If you need to, write down the prayer on a piece of paper and hold it in front of you in order to get the wording correct. Sitting or standing with your spine erect and your body relaxed, say aloud something like this:

"Great I AM/I AM Father, I AM requesting as your child and my Divine Birthright that you release to me your Sacred Fire to purify my mind, emotions, and body. Release me from all sense addictions, restore my Divine powers, and resurrect and immortalize my body in this lifetime. I command this Sacred Fire to be anchored in, through, and around me permanently and to continuously work without interruption until I have achieved my Ascension."

Then sit quietly for at least thirty minutes. During this time, it is important to feel and visualize the Sacred Fire descending into your body, saturating every cell, and creating a flame all around you that goes out about six feet in all directions. Hold this flame in your mind and become one with it. See all the colors of the Fire and breathe them into your body. Breathing is a very powerful way to energize and anchor the power. The Fire is limitless, and as you breathe deeply, see and feel this fire saturating all of your body; breathe it into your pores and cells—not just into your nose.

After the activation ceremony, mediate twice daily for at least 20 minutes, charging and strengthening the Fire, and you will begin to feel these energizing sessions. Draw the Fire in through your skin, down from the top of your head, and into all parts of your body. Some of the sensations you may feel are tingling, waves, spinning, prickly needles, lightheadedness, strong surges down your spine, pulsations on your forehead, jerks and twitches, to name a few. After you have spent 10 minutes breathing in the Fire, relax and allow the Fire to radiate and begin to work for another 10 minutes. To reinforce this action, affirm aloud, or in your mind, the following:

"I AM commanding the Sacred Fire to consume all my discord, addictions, and human qualities, and replace them with perfect peace, wisdom, love, health, and abundance. This Fire is permanently anchored within me and protects me forever, Amen. So be it."

Working with the Sacred Fire. In the

beginning, you will need to use strong will and determination to change your patterns, but the more you work with the Fire, the easier it gets. If you do not have a strong will, it is best to get with others or join a group to help you over this initial hurdle. You are pushing against lifetimes of addictive patterns, and the more energy you can produce, the faster you can break through the current.

The Sacred Fire's energy can be subtle in the body and you may not feel it all the time. In meditation sessions, however, you may feel gentle rocking motions or waves of emotions, as it is cleansing out the old patterns. Sometimes, you can feel radiation emanating off your body and, during sessions that are more powerful, it can actually feel like the energy is pushing into your skin and pores. You may feel pressure underneath the skin; this is because toxins and imperfections are pushing their way out of the body. There may be a slight achy feeling in your muscles and bones, but just relax, and it will pass. These are emotional, mental, and physical toxins that we have created, which are being released.

When the Fire is in a realignment session, there can be more dramatic body sensations. It is important during this time not to panic or have any fear. You must trust that your I AM Father and this Sacred Fire will not harm you. It is pure love and, thus, cannot do anything but create perfection. During a realignment session, the I AM Father is beginning to anchor the new blueprint body into the old one. As the old gives way to the new, it may cause friction. The Fire will express itself as a spinning vortex of energy, usually focusing on one part of your spine. During a session, the Fire may focus on the lower area of your spine around the solar plexus. You will feel a spinning sensation going around and inside your body in just this one area—the rest of your body is unaffected. Sometimes the vortex energy can be so powerful as to move the entire body in a back-and-forth movement. During these realignment sessions, usually activated by long intense meditations, the Fire can travel up and down your spine. The vortex often focuses on the heart area and the spinning sensation will surround your chest and penetrate into your heart. On many occasions, it will concentrate on just your head area and, when this happens, your head may move from left to right in a fast motion.

Again, it is imperative not to be afraid; this is just the Sacred Fire realigning your energy fields to be in harmony with the higher light patterns and not the fallen dark ones. If, at any time, you feel uncomfortable or just want to stop the session, simply say to the energy, *"Okay stop,"* and it will obey. Also please note, these body movements are not something *you* do; if *you* are doing it, it is not the Sacred Fire at work.

Once in a while, you can have a major re-alignment session in which the entire body is engulfed in a strong spinning pattern and your whole body is shaking. The torso will rock in a back-and-forth motion, and your head may have a spinning motion. The energy *always* spins from left to right around your body, not from right to left. You can even *hear* the energy, as it spins around your body. It sounds like you are in a wind tunnel, but the wind is rhythmic in nature.

Then, as suddenly as the spinning began, it will simply stop, and this will tell you the session is over. It is important that you sit still or lie down, because you will feel light-headed or have a spacey feeling for a short while. After one of these sessions, you will now have more purified light in your body than before, which strengthens your connection to the I AM Father.

Because the newly saturated light does not desire nor need the things of the world to exist, it helps you break addictive patterns. The more realignment sessions you have, the easier it gets to break addictions. I have activated these alignment sessions in people, and once you have achieved certain stability with the Fire, you can activate others as well. Saints who did not eat food actually lived on this Light substance. The Fire will slowly start to transform your body–gradually–throughout your life, so you can continue to develop mastery over the physical world.

If you are a person with a strong sexual desire, this Fire will help balance and channel that energy, so you can use it in ways that are more creative.

If your purpose is to work in the healing arts, you may receive a portion of the Sacred Fire to use to restore and heal others.

When receiving the healing portion of the Fire, you will notice a very distinct feeling. During a meditation session, it is a good idea to place your hands on your knees with palms up and opened in a relaxed fashion. The Fire will descend directly into your palms in a spiral-like motion. First, you may feel a pressure of energy building up between your hands, arms, and chest area, as if a large beach-ball was being placed in your lap. The pressure will build and feel like it is pushing against your body. Then a very real and tangible energy will begin to enter into your palms in a spiral motion.

When this first happened to me in meditation, I opened my eyes and began to watch the energy. The fact that you are analytically evaluating the energy in no way diminishes or interferes with its action. One way you will know that you are not imagining or creating it yourself is that it goes on working *no matter what you are thinking*. In my case, as I moved my hands up and down, this spiraling energy kept entering into my hands. When I turned my hands toward each other, a strong pressure built up between my arms and began to pulsate.

Even if you cannot see the energy with your eyes, you will definitely feel it. Once you have anchored enough of this aspect of the Fire, you can simply command the energy to come forth. It will pour out of your hands to wherever you wish. You can even do long-distance healings.

If your intent is to use the Sacred Fire to heal, rejuvenate, and purify your physical body, begin by invoking the Fire and giving it a command. For example, *"By the power of the Great I AM, I invoke the Sacred Fire to youth and rejuvenate my physical body."* Use this decree everyday. However, if you wish to concentrate the energy for more intense work, follow this guideline:

In meditation, stretch out your hands and, invoking the fire, command it to pour its rejuvenating energy through your hands. Wait until you feel the surge or spiral energy, and then place your hands directly on the area you wish to heal. If you want to remove cancer from your body, place your hands on the area and command the Fire to annihilate the cancer and heal your body. *Please do not fret and get discouraged if you do not see immediate results*. The more you are able to feel the energy, the stronger your results will be.

It is also important to remember that your physical body is the outer shield to the world. It takes all the abuse—both physically, emotionally and mentally, so it is extremely difficult not to have some kind of ailment or aging. Even the most positive person undergoes the stresses of the world, and the body absorbs those stresses because it is a part of the physical world. Remember, most people resurrect—which means they had to die of something in the first place. *Therefore, the most important law or action you can do to guarantee your immortality and eventual ascension is an intent-motive-desire based on love.*

Many people who died are later resurrected because they had a pure heart, clean spiritual motives, and had released sufficient attachments. The Great I AM realized how difficult overcoming the physical senses would be—that is why we were given the Sacred Fire. This incorruptible Fire has many qualities, but, most importantly, it has a purifying and releasing quality called the Violet Flame. Without its power, we would forever be chained to our addictions.

The History of the Sacred Fire. In the past, people working with the Fire isolated themselves in retreats far away from the desires of the world. Over time, they managed to free themselves of addictions and resurrect or immortalize their bodies. Recently, however, the Counsels of Light decided to establish the Sacred Fire on Earth in much the same fashion as on other planets. On many of the previous Separatist planets, there were temples where large concentrations of the Sacred Fire existed, and individuals were able to use that fire. Once a certain percentage of the population on those planets used the Sacred Fire, transformation came quickly to the planet.

In recent years, the Counsels have decided to enact a campaign to teach humanity more about the Sacred Fire, so that we too can free ourselves from our addictions and regain our powers. When Jesus ascended, he chose to "return" to Earth and, with other Immortals, help each of us attain the same victory.

If you are able to work with others who are

using the Sacred Fire, either in a group or in a family, this will increase the intensity and power of the Sacred Fire. When new people join the group, they will experience a faster activation and acceleration in their growth because the group will have created a powerful vortex of the Fire. I have been told that many of us will be able to go into large gatherings and activate hundreds or thousands of people at one time. In this way, the people of Earth have the same potential to transform their reality as the populations of other planets.

I wish everyone could spend one evening with the Immortals and see what I have seen. Compared to them, we act like depraved animals. If we truly understood the contrast, we would spend every waking moment using the Sacred Fire to purify and cleanse this world.

There is also a protective quality in the Fire, and the more you anchor it into your world, the more it transforms and purifies everything around you. This naturally keeps your world more harmonious, because those situations that are in discord are dissolved or

removed from your life. Once the discord is

removed, regaining your natural spiritual powers becomes easier. Then it is only a matter of time before you achieve the full victory and live with others who are already in the Golden Age.

ECSTASY OF THE FIRE

In stillness I wait, a gentle breeze cools my
face.

My lover comes to take me up in his embrace.

Bells tolling, I hear a soft calling, it sounds like a
faint Echo—softer yet louder as he approaches.

WAIT! WAIT! I am not ready—but it is too late.

He has pierced mine heart with his rays of love,
oh so great,

A love I cannot bear—I seek to hold on to myself, But it is in vain; he has raptured me,

Pulled from my body, soaring high and
free.

Oh! I have died such a pleasant death—
The death of love's embrace.

Resurrection and Ascension

Some of the driving beliefs throughout the philosophies and religions of the world have been the belief in eternal life, resurrection, and immortality. The promise of these events motivates us to worship and live a good life. Intellectuals argue that the belief in eternal life is a fantasy created to pacify our misery while keeping us under control and civilized. Without the hope of an eternal life filled with joy, immortality, and love, humanity would live in utter despair. The mess we have created would be our only existence, and, it is feared, civilization itself would become utter chaos.

Thus, most religions use the idea of eternal life, in either heaven or hell, to instill obedience and keep the masses in line. If the masses fear eternal punishment and damnation, they will certainly live a good and decent life and, therefore, be easier to control and manipulate. When people long for a paradise with vestal virgins and life abundant, they can be persuaded to do anything in order to achieve their individual entry into that paradise. Religions, throughout time, have been the greatest source of evil and wars that this planet has ever known. Perhaps now, in the twenty-first century, the masses are ready to put aside irrational, fear-based dogmas and, in place of them, develop self-discipline, maturity, and spiritual awareness.

Resurrections and ascensions are based on practical laws and science. The mystery surrounding the process should not be based on superstitious fears or *supernatural* events. In fact, the process is quite *natural* and in accordance with scientific laws. The fact that our current civilization is unaware of this science does not prove the absence of it. History has proven what is mysterious and supernatural in one age, becomes normal science in a new age. It is fitting that we begin this new millennium unmasking the mysteries of resurrection and ascension and applying our disciplined mind to proving their reality. Until we put the effort into applying these laws and proving the results, how will we ever make the unknown—known, and the supernatural—natural?

I wish I could tell you that I have personally ascended, and that I am here to give you a step-by-step guide to the process. I know there are those who claim to be Ascended Masters; they say they have reincarnated to help poor ignorant humanity. All of these claims are false. These people are steeped in their own self-centeredness and need to be regarded by the masses as "special." *No Ascended Master ever reincarnates back into a Separatist body.* The Masters have shattered that blueprint, and it is no longer a part of them. What a Master can and often do, however, is manifest a temporary physical body that we can see in order to interact with us on a daily basis.

The Immortals and Ascended Masters are our elder brothers and sisters who have freed themselves from the addictions of the physical body, mastered the laws of nature, and defeated death. They are not to be worshiped as gods in the sense that they are unique and beyond us. *Those Masters who have remained on Earth are here because they desire to help us achieve the same thing*. Many of us have known these Immortal Masters in previous lives before they ascended and, thus, have close ties with them. I have had the opportunity to meet a few of them, but that does not mean I am any more unique than anyone else. I am full of flaws and shortcomings. Perhaps I have had the good fortune of working through most of my addictions and can be more receptive to their existence, but anyone can achieve this if their desire is strong enough. The Immortal Masters can appear as normal and relaxed as anyone you might meet on the street, or they can appear in all their glory as great and powerful Beings.

Immortals

Immortals are people born in the normal way, but through unwavering intent and self-discipline, they have been able to break all attachments to physical addictions. Once freed from the distractions of form, their latent spiritual powers begin to develop, and they begin the immortalization process. If they die before it is complete, they are resurrected using the Sacred Fire. Some of their spiritual powers involve the ability to communicate with all living things, demonstrating a oneness with man, animals, and nature. This synergetic oneness gives them the ability to work in harmony with their environment. With all resistance gone, even gravity does not work against them. The result is a rejuvenation of the physical body and instantaneous travel. They are true masters of their environment.

Over time, they no longer need any food to maintain their existence; they live off the Sacred Fire. They are masters of time and space and can disappear at will. In addition, Earth's laws (which are corrupt) do not bind them, and as a result, all their desires manifest instantly. Having regained their original identity as Rays of Light, their bodies vibrate at a slightly higher vibration of light than ours do.

In the past, many Rays of Light isolated themselves from the Separatists deep inside mountain ranges. Even today, some of these places still exist. Immortals that are thousands of years old and some that have just attained immortality live in these cities. Our practical minds cannot believe this because we have explored the interior of mountains and seen nothing but rock. However, remember all the miraculous things that Jesus did during his time in the public, such as walking on water and controlling the Powers of Nature.

These Immortals have the ability to shield their existence from prying eyes by simply raising the vibration of their dwellings to just slightly above our visible light spectrum. Also, they can cloak themselves in a shield of invisibility similar to the alien space ships that visit our planet.

I, myself, experienced a spontaneous dematerialization (disappearance from the visible light spectrum) once while using the Sacred Fire. Upstairs one evening, while deep in meditation and sitting on my bedroom floor, the Fire began to do something to me I had never felt before. A strong pressure that tingled within my bones and muscles began. It felt as if this pressure was pushing its way outward. Soon this tingling pressure reached my skin and caused me to open my eyes.

I looked to see what was happening because I felt as if I might explode or come unglued from the inside out. This did not hurt in any way, but it gave me a feeling of some great force pushing from within the cells of my body. I saw, in my mind's eye, the cells of my body begin to dissolve their structure. I massaged my arms and legs but the feeling continued, so I tried to remain calm. Next, I had the thought of acceleration and, suddenly, there was nothing but tiny golden light particles everywhere. My consciousness was completely unaltered—but my physical body had disappeared!

I then had some kind of vision because I was able to look all around me. I could see the outline of what were walls, consisting of tiny golden particles held close together by what I somehow knew was thought-magnetism. Everywhere else, the particles floated freely in space—billions of them. My consciousness traveled around the house looking at what I knew were familiar objects that were no longer solid; everything was just a trace outline of its former self. This was also true with the outside environment such as the trees and plants. Interestingly, though, I tried to see my body, and there was nothing there.

The faint outlines that existed on everything else did not exist on my body; I was the golden light particles blended into all the other free-floating particles everywhere around me. I am not sure how long I was in this state, but after a period of time, I began to sense a slowing down. In the next moment I was standing in my downstairs living room. This coalescing stage was instant and I felt perfectly normal, except for being a little light-headed.

Later, one of the Immortals explained to me that when a person dematerializes, the electrons accelerate their spin, tightening. This increases the light quotient in the atoms and particles of the physical body. The cell walls and dense mass can no longer maintain their shape and simply give way to a higher frequency light.

When a person rematerializes, the opposite occurs, in that the light particles slow down and become denser, eventually reforming the magnetized thought of the physical body. All physical objects are held together by thought or consciousness. This consciousness designs a blueprint of its desire and then projects its will or intent into the blueprint making it solid. I was told that because my consciousness was freed from material addictions, the de-materialization process was allowed so I might have the experience of my true nature.

A belief in Immortals is easier to support than many imagine. Everything in our manifested universe is made of some frequency or vibration of light; even the densest matter is light. Light exists here as different frequencies and waves. There is visible light that we see with our eyes and also x-rays, gamma rays, and microwave rays. Thought itself is a form of light. There are also waves of light such as radio and television. While we cannot see radio waves, with the right science, we can hear them.

It is the same with other frequencies of light; with the right understanding, we can access these frequencies as well. The more we shed our addictions to this physical form of light, the easier it will be to see and communicate with other forms of light. Look back throughout history; there have always been people who could see and/or communicate with angels, saints, departed loved ones, and many other Beings.

The reason most Immortals and Ascended Masters do not make their presence known to the average person is that most people would react with either fear or god-worship. Their level of existence is so far advanced from ours; it is literally god-like to the average person.

Jesus is a perfect example; his powers so frightened the current religions of the time, he was crucified, while the masses worshiped him as the only son of God. Their logic being that God–a male–begat only one offspring–a male–and sent that only offspring to one particular planet, among zillions of planets, to redeem a small group of people in the Mediterranean.

This may have been a good story for the tribal mentalities of the time, but we are much too smart and advanced, by now, to keep perpetuating such fairy tales. The only reason the belief still exists is that the religions of the world are addicted to power and control.

When people stop being so fearful, more of the Immortals will make themselves known. They are only going to reveal their identity to people who have attained some level of self-discipline and spiritual awakening. What purpose would it serve to reveal themselves if we are not able to understand them? It would be like college professors trying to teach kindergarteners. Most of humanity would want to either kill them or worship them. The Immortals want neither. *What they want are people who are done with the attractions of the physical world and are ready to transcend them.*

People who are still caught up in wanting to be loved, wanting to have things, wanting success, wanting children, and wanting power are not ready to meet the masters. They will have to settle for ordinary people pointing the way to a better life.

Immortals can spend hundreds of years in their bodies working among humanity. They have been known to influence heads of state, governments, industry, and people of influence without their identity ever being known. Many of them have bank accounts with vast sums of money that they use to influence world events. Some own large estates and homes throughout the world. Many have businesses, are quite active, can blend in with any culture, and speak any language at will.

I know one Immortal who is a wealthy Buddhist businessman. He owns an island where he has built a small private resort. Visiting the resort is by invitation only, but many people other than Immortals have stayed there. You may have met an Immortal and not even known it! By the way, Buddhism is a good path for releasing your attachments to the world.

Immortals operate as middle management in the governing of this planet and Ascended Masters like Jesus are the upper management. Spiritually advanced mortals are the lower level. Many Immortals could make their ascension, but choose to stay in physical form to be more accessible to humanity. They can gain a greater understanding of the times they are living in if they stay in physical form.

Even today, if you shot bullets into an Immortal and was assured by our current science that he had died, an Immortal would simply rise up and walk away. In our original state—before we became attached to our physical form—we were in harmony with all things, we could shape shift and dissolve our bodies. Everything around us was subject to change according to our will.

Immortals, too, are one with everything. They can walk through fire, drink toxins, walk on water, and do anything else they desire. To them, all of these things and events are just patterns of light, which they control. Yet even in *this* advanced state, Immortals can, occasionally, experience upsetting emotions that influence their judgment. Not until they have ascended are they completely free from the influence of the physical worlds. They spend a large part of their time keeping the Separatist Dark Brotherhood from totally dominating the planet.

Resurrection

Just as Jesus called Lazarus back to life, Immortals can resurrect someone who has just passed through death. In a resurrection process, the person passes through death and, while separated from his body, he is met by an Immortal or Ascended Master. Using the Sacred Fire, they dissolve the last vestiges of addicted patterns and this frees the body from the Separatist reality. They are restored to perfect youth and health.

The possibility of other resurrections is even mentioned in the Bible. In Matthew, Chapter 10:7–8, Jesus says to his disciples, "*The Kingdom of Heaven is at hand, cure the sick, **raise the dead**, cleanse lepers, and drive out demons.*" Based on this statement alone, we can assume there are Immortals living among us. After all, what was the purpose of raising Lazarus and others from the dead if not to continue to live on Earth in their original bodies? Why not let them die and go to a marvelous place called heaven?

It seems a horrible thing to do to someone—bring them back to life to live in this miserable existence of pain and suffering. The only logical explanation behind this action is that *when they were raised from the dead, they were no longer affected by the world. They were in the world, but not a part of it.*

Death is the strongest attachment we have because everywhere around us, our reality reflects the passing of time through death. This is an illusion propagated by our corrupted physical form. It does not matter how spiritually evolved the saints, gurus, and spiritual leaders have been; most of them have died because of this one belief. What we do not know, however, is how many of them may have been resurrected after dying.

Magical resurrections do not have the same results. When a person or animal is magically resurrected, the magician is using borrowed light from within himself or others to reanimate the person or animal's body. When the person or animal comes back to life, they are the same, as before death, with all their flaws and personality. Such people or animals are living on borrowed time. Eventually, when the light exhausts itself, they will go through another death.

Many Black Magicians can draw off the energy from the larvae attached to people and use this to reanimate a body. Others who use magic as a source of good to help others will use their own light to reanimate an animal or person. There have been incidents where someone resurrected a family pet only to lose them a month later when a car runs over them. Borrowed light has only a short span because it is not coming from the

Sacred Fire of the I AM. It is more like recycled energy; only the Fire's effects are permanent.

Some people manage to bypass both death and resurrection by immortalizing their bodies through alchemical processes. These processes involve special elixirs and tinctures, which are created using not only physical ingredients, but also, most importantly, the essential ingredient of the Sacred Fire.

Consuming this tincture slowly, over time, restores youth and immortalizes the body, and the experience of death never occurs. The Comte de Saint Germain, who was known as the "Wonderman of Europe," immortalized his body in this way; only later did he achieve his ascension. Many people have tried to duplicate this alchemical tincture, which some think is a white powder, but without the Sacred Fire, they never achieve the immortalizing results. Since most alchemists and magicians are still caught up in physical addictions, they are nowhere near ready for immortality. A person will not be able to achieve immortality until he has achieved a significant level of personal mastery.

Ascension

Ascensions happen only after a person has become an Immortal. One must spend time as an Immortal developing skills and mastering his environment. Some of the skills developed are: de-materialization and teleportation of the body; creating anything one desires, instantly, from thought into the physical; healing and resurrecting the dead; controlling the Elementals and Powers of Nature; mastering the use of the Sacred Fire; and assisting the Ascended Masters with the evolution of humanity.

Every Immortal, when he is ready, goes through a sacred ascension ceremony. This is performed with several Ascended Masters using a specific aspect of the Sacred Fire. In this ceremony, the Immortal is surrounded by Ascended Masters, and while standing in the center, he invokes the Sacred Fire. The Ascended Masters create a temporary vortex of protective energy while the Immortal is going through the transformation process.

He must have developed the ability to activate this powerful aspect of the Fire in order to complete his ascension.

Once the Sacred Fire is activated, it begins the final dissolving process of the old blueprint. When complete, the Immortal now lives in a new body capable of existing not only in the realms of light, but also in the realms of thought.

Once anchored in the new body, he will never again succumb to the physical attractions of the worlds of light, because he has transcended them through wisdom and spiritual maturity. This means, as an Ascended Master, he can now travel to all the physical worlds by thought and rematerialize a new body specific for that world. However, now when he manifests any physical form, it will have the energetic or magnetic blueprint of his Creator as an invincible seal of protection. This seal, along with the wisdom the Master gained while in the worlds of separation, assures that he will never lose his identity again. When he is not in the worlds of light and matter, he can exist in the realms of thought.

Each Ray of the original Twin Rays must go through this process. Since one of the Twin Rays will usually achieve immortality or ascension before the other, the Ascended Ray will then spend their time helping their Twin.

Twin Rays vs. Soul Mates

Generally speaking, the nature of Twin Rays has been misunderstood. Many people think they are soul mates, but they are two different things. Soul mates are people with whom you have spent hundreds of lifetimes with; they are very familiar with your addictions, and therefore, more compatible with you. A person can have dozens of soul mates and interact with many of them in just one lifetime.

Twin Rays, however, rarely incarnate at the same time. One Twin usually works from the spiritual realms as a guide for the other in the physical realm. They can blend their thoughts more easily when one Twin is not in a physical body. When one is more advanced than the other and reaches immortality or ascension first, their power to influence and help the other is greatly increased. It is a blessing to the unascended Twin to have his other half ascended, because this influence can greatly accelerate the unascended Twin's progress.

Purgatory and Astral Ascensions

Another way ascension is achieved follows along the Catholic belief system or what John the writer of Revelations was trying to comprehend. Unfortunately, the Catholic faith does not understand the original teachings and, therefore, have contaminated the truth with their own fears. The truth is that in certain situations where people have detached from the addictions of the physical body and have passed through the death process, they will remain in Purgatory or the Astral Realms and not reincarnate.

There are many levels of growth in these nonphysical realms, which are just as real as life on Earth. In many of these realms, there are cities filled with people living their lives in much the same way they did on Earth. Some of these realms are filled with people addicted to lust, greed, murder, and the like.

In the purest of these realms, there are people who have released almost all of their addictions and are living in peace and beauty.

Many of our great science fiction and fantasy novels are written about kingdoms in the astral plane, such as J.R.R. Tolkien's *Lord of the Rings* trilogy. People have often referred to these places as the seven levels of Heaven, or upper and lower Astral; the lower levels being Hell and the upper levels being Heaven. However, this is not the true Heaven where Jesus lives, and is still attached to Earth.

The fires of Hell and Purgatory are actually the Sacred Fires. These Fires do not, in any way, torture or burn those who use them. *The only misery and suffering that occurs in the lower regions of the astral or purgatory is done by the souls living there to each other.* Ascended Masters and Rays of Light (what we call angels) work in these lower realms using the Sacred Fire to purify the different kingdoms and realms. Each realm has a place where the Sacred Fire is always burning and, in these areas, people can come of their own free will and dwell in the fire, cleansing and purifying themselves. I, myself, have escorted disincarnated souls to these safe areas for purifying and have even taken a number of demons to the Sacred Fires.

An example of someone who died and did not have to reincarnate would be Sri Yukteswar, the Guru of Paramahansa Yogananda who is written about in the book, *Autobiography of a Yogi*. After his death, he was offered the opportunity to stay in the Astral realms and teach those who were there. He accepted this opportunity and came to visit Yogananda in a physical body to show him that he had overcome death. Yogananda held him in his arms and talked to him for several hours about the astral worlds. Incidentally, Yogananda is also living in the spiritual realms. When I visited him in an out-of-body trip, he had established a school much like the one he had on Earth and was teaching many souls during their waiting period.

Perhaps another example, although it is not documented, would be saints such as Saint

Francis, who have abandoned the physical world and demonstrated spiritual powers. People who have healed and performed miracles might be the types that, after death, are offered the opportunity to stay in the Astral/Purgatory realms and not reincarnate. They are given the choice to perform service and acquire mastery of the Sacred Fire in the nonphysical worlds. They act as guides and teachers to souls in the astral realms and people who request their help here on Earth. After spending time mastering their skills, they are offered the opportunity to ascend from the upper realms into the true Heaven or Ascended Realms where Jesus and the other Ascended Ones live.

These Astral Ascension Ceremonies are performed in much the same way. The Sacred Fire is used to dissolve the blueprint of the old corrupted body. Even though you do not have a "worldly" body, you have a physical body attached to that realm of light. That body or *astral body* is still part of the corrupted Separatist blueprint. (The astral body is also the body that one uses when traveling in the dream worlds or out-of-body experiences). This ceremony activates the new blueprint body and the individual "ascends" into it. *This is the only way to escape reincarnation.* As long as the old blueprint body exists, you must use it for reincarnation. Ascension is the only process that dissolves the old blueprint and frees you from its patterns. Once you have achieved ascension, you live in the true Heaven or Golden Age.

Enlightenment

The term "enlightenment" describes people who, while on Earth, have restored communication with their I AM Parent. This is often called God-Realization, Self-Realization, union with God, bliss, and "living in the now." All this refers to is reconnecting to your Divine nature. The separation that was originally created has been overcome, and the person has "come home" to a place that was always there. *Enlightenment is simply returning home to your original identity.* Thus, a person can be "enlightened" and still have to reincarnate. *Enlightenment is only one part of mastery; it is the part that provides the Knowingness of who we are.* Once a person knows who they are, they have the confidence to express and develop their spiritual abilities. The key is in *knowing* who you are; for when you have this vital brick in your foundation, you are on the path to immortality.

A person who has "become enlightened" has his or her own personality and hundreds of lifetimes of developed abilities. They express themselves in different ways and are not all the quiet, meditative, soft-spoken people who live in caves or monasteries. Some can be very outgoing, outspoken, movers and shakers; it all depends upon their purpose.

Many work on personal mastery quietly, while others tend to draw groups of seekers. Being enlightened, you still have flaws and make mistakes, as mentioned earlier; even Immortals can lose their tempers. *It is not until you have completely ascended from the lower blueprint of desires that you can consider yourself perfect.*

It should be evident by now: enlightenment, immortality, and ascension are very personal events that are not achieved en masse. The New Age culture believes extraterrestrials or legions of angels are going to appear and suddenly transform everyone on the planet and usher in a physical Golden Age. The obstacle to this event is that not everyone on the planet *wants* this to happen. Many are perfectly content to live their lives enjoying all that the physical world has to offer. Unfortunately, it usually takes a catastrophic event brought on by accumulated human discord to shock people out of their ruts and belief systems.

The Dark or Separatists want to keep us all in a trance—addicted to our televisions, sports, drugs, gambling, sex, money, and/or children. The more they entangle us in the web of emotions, the less likely we are to think for ourselves, much less free ourselves.

Immortal Encounters

The good news is that more resurrections and ascensions are happening everyday, and many Immortals are choosing to stay behind and interact with humanity. They are usually involved with specific projects that deal with trouble spots on the planet.

I have had various types of encounters with Immortals. Some introduced themselves as such; others are incognito. I remember one day I had been running errands and had not eaten. I decided to stop by a health food restaurant about 11:00 in the morning. I ordered a sandwich and sat down to eat. Most of the tables were empty, but soon a young dark-skinned Indian woman entered and ordered lunch. I was browsing through a magazine as I ate when I heard her ask if she could sit down with me. I thought it was a little odd considering the entire place was empty, but then I determined that she must want some company and agreed.

We made polite conversation, and then she asked me about the classes I was teaching. I looked rather puzzled, since I had not mentioned that I taught any classes. I began discussing them; she was very interested in my understanding of immortality and ascension and asked many insightful questions. These questions actually helped me gain a great deal of clarity. During this time, she never ate a single thing from her plate. Soon I was finished with lunch and said goodbye to her.

I had one more errand for the day, which

was to grocery shop at Whole Foods. With cart in hand, I headed down an aisle and, as I made the turn into the next aisle, there stood my Indian friend with a cart full of groceries! I was shocked and bewildered; I had left her at the restaurant with a full lunch to eat. How had she managed to arrive before me and done all that shopping? She stood there calmly staring straight into my eyes and, suddenly, the fog lifted from my mind. I *knew* she was an Immortal. In that brief second of recognition, she made the bend into the next aisle. I darted after her, but when I turned the corner, she was gone, *vanished*, cart and all.

Another time, I was teaching a seminar at a New Age Fair in Colorado. I had been assigned a room at the top of the stairs in an old school house. In between lectures, I happened to be standing outside the room with a clear view of the stairs and the front door. A young man walked in, climbed the stairs, and walked directly to me. He had beautiful eyes and a wonderful mischievous smile. He began to ask about my lectures. We had a lively discussion and, in the end, he told me how pleased he was with my teaching, and that he needed to be back at Mount Shasta within the hour (Mount Shasta is a mountain located in northern California).

I responded to him by saying, "*There is no way you can get back to Mount Shasta in an hour, much less anytime soon, not from Colorado.*" He just smiled, walked down the stairs, opened the door, turned back to me, and winked. In that instant, I knew he was the great Ascended Master Saint Germain who is known to frequent Mt. Shasta! This time, I literally jumped down the stairs, but by the time I got to the doors and out to the outer steps, he was gone. There was no sign of him anywhere, even though I looked all around the building. During the rest of the seminar, I asked everyone I came across if they had seen this man; no one had.

This was not the first time I had met Saint Germain in the physical world. My first physical encounter, when I knew who he was, took place when I was 31 years old. At the time, I was still a Southern Baptist, but had started visiting a new church called Unity. Unity had a bookstore, and I had been browsing one Sunday when, from the top shelf, a book literally fell on my head. I was new to metaphysics, reincarnation, and anything spiritual, as far as books were concerned. Yes, I had gained knowledge from traveling in the spirit worlds, but I had assumed no one knew anything about this information but me, which was pretty naive of me at the time.

The Beings I talked with never told me to go read this or that book, so I did not realize others knew some of the things I knew. I decided God must want me to read this book, so I climbed up the ladder and got the second volume as well. These two books, *Unveiled Mysteries* and *The Magic Presence,* confirmed some of what I had been experiencing. They also provided new information that I was thrilled to know was readily available in the physical world.

Halfway into the second volume, I had an amazing experience. Late one night as I slept, the room became charged with an electrical energy that woke me up. I sat up in bed, and there was a blue hue everywhere. Suddenly, standing at the foot of my bed was the Ascended Master Saint Germain. I was stunned! As he was holding my copy of the book, *The Magic Presence*, he said he had been waiting for the right time for us to be properly introduced. He mentioned that we had worked together for a very long time and were good friends. Suddenly, he threw the book up into the air, and it burst into a million particles of light. While I was watching the light particles, he disappeared. I was so excited; I got up and stood on the site where he had stood. Eventually, I went back to bed and, in the morning, I found my book sitting at the foot of my bed—intact.

You can have encounters in all kinds of places. It might be when you are riding a ski lift or walking in the park. It can seem like a casual, normal conversation with someone, but afterwards, you are often left with a new perspective on things. On occasion, they will even reveal who they are. The physical age at which you encounter these Beings does not matter. I encountered them even when I was a child.

Often, they talked to me about personal problems, people, and world events. Once, I remember that they physically interceded for me when I was visiting a relative. When I was about 8 years old, I was sleeping on the top bunk bed in their guest room. I rolled off the bed in the middle of the night only to be caught in midair by a beautiful Being. He held me in his arms for a moment, then stood me up on the floor, and instructed me to sleep on the bottom bunk thereafter.

Immortals are quite willing to communicate with people who have let go of their fears and who have the will and discipline to achieve freedom. They have told me that, over the next few decades, they want to open the door to their world and make it more mainstream, much like books, television, and movies have done concerning Extraterrestrials and Angels.

America's Destiny

Because I cannot help but be influenced by the current terrorist events of our time, I have written about America and her destiny.

The United States of America has, from the beginning, been under the guidance of Ascended Masters and Immortals. The purpose for creating America was to provide a safe haven where freedom and spiritual discovery could be nourished without fear of persecution. Because this planet has so many belief systems and levels of spiritual awareness, there needed to be a place where spiritual exploration could flourish and, eventually, produce an awakened population ready to rejoin their brothers and sisters in the universe.

As it currently stands, America is the guardian of freedom for the planet. This includes the people born on Earth, those in the astral realms, and many of the "aliens" who use Earth as a refuge. Because of this, the Dark Brotherhood is using all of their powers to keep the truth from reaching the masses. They have created elaborate systems to agitate our emotions such as violent entertainment, pitting one part of the population against the other, and keeping us in a perpetual state of confusion. The last thing they want is truth and clarity. Currently, many changes need to take place in order to create an environment ready to meet the Immortals and Ascended Masters en masse.

First, *all* fundamental religions that instill fear and repression must be transformed. This includes the Jewish, Christian, and Muslim faiths, and any philosophy that plays into the hands of the Dark Separatists. In the current struggle with Islam, it is very essential that extreme Muslims not be allowed to spread their doctrine.

Nine months before the last presidential election, I was attending meetings in the retreats with the Ascended Masters when I saw the then-Governor Bush in a meeting. The Masters were discussing the presidency with him, and the huge responsibility he would carry in holding the light of freedom for the world. Until 9-ll, President Bush had not met his full destiny. Yet his single purpose for having been born, at this time, was to secure the base of freedom, the United

States, and then begin the process of eliminating the dark threats against it.

Unfortunately, America has always been the target for the Dark Forces because they know its existence heralds their ultimate demise. The plan of the Dark in World War II was to gain all of Europe, and use it as a staging base to destroy America. America and her allies' victory put the Dark at bay for the time being, but the Dark never rest. Over time, they gained momentum and found new areas on Earth to incite hatred towards her. America's involvement in World War II was necessary in order to remove Evil from the planet and allow the Light to reestablish itself in those areas of the world.

The Ascended Ones' focus is now on the Muslim countries and the transformation of that part of the world. We are in a critical time in our history, and President Bush is being guided by the Ascended Masters, particularly Jesus. This does not mean that Bush does not have faults or other agendas. The Immortals have seen many a President come and go; they are working with a flawed humanity in order to accomplish the greater good.

If you take an honest look at those countries that support terrorism, you can easily discern that they are steeped in darkness. Most of these countries have vast amounts of wealth, yet what have they produced? Not one world-class university or hospital, not one incredible, life-transforming invention or new technology. They only manage to fund and produce terrorists, and their people are living in tribal mentalities. This is exactly what the Dark wants, addictions to power and control, suppression and ignorance. Even though all countries have some of these problems, the terrorist countries have shown susceptibility for mass indoctrination, much like when Hitler used mind control on the masses in Germany. Unfortunately, the perfect vehicle for any kind of mind control is religion.

When I was visiting India, I was amazed to see that most Hindu Indians only had a few children. However, the Muslim Indians married off their girls as soon as they were menstruating (around 12–13 years old) to start them reproducing. Each girl was giving birth to as many as 8 to 12 children. These children were then put out into the streets to beg. I asked an Indian government official about this situation, and he told me the Muslims have an agenda to dominate the globe through large populations. The Christians also have their form of mind control, but because the Ascended Master Jesus is the source of that religion, the Dark is predominantly diminished. The Light is the strongest element in that faith. Now is the time we need courage and strong convictions to deal with the terrorist threat.

I realize many in the New Age have a problem with war and would rather live and let live, but we should read the lessons given in the Indian Bhagavad-Gita which tells of a great battle between good and evil. The warrior Arjuna, whose greatest strength was his noble- ness of spirit and love for his fellow man, stands upon a battlefield ready for war. He is unable to fight because his mind and his heart are in a terrible conflict. His mind knows, as the protector of freedom and civilization, what he must do, but his heart is filled with compassion for his enemy. He does not wish to kill them, so he is in conflict with himself. The Immortal Lord Krishna, who was at his side, explains to him that man is the master of his own destiny, and that this battle is merely God playing out the struggle of separation verses union. Lord Krishna explains that no one really dies; they merely change form and begin all over again until they finally learn the lessons of love. Krishna reprimands Arjuna not to let his emotions overrule his mind, as the mind knows its duty, which is to protect that which is good and desires peace.

The United States has to use military action as a last resort in order to eliminate the greater threat. The old saying, *"When enough good people lie down and do nothing, evil prevails"* is very true; *we cannot allow the Dark to extinguish the Light on this planet.* The question in any action, as explained earlier, is our *motive* and *intent*. Our desire should be to protect those we love and to do it without hate and vengeance. Yet, our emotions should not guide our actions; they should be tempered by our disciplined mind, which is doing its duty.

Those whose emotions are undisciplined and chained to fear are easily led. Clever minds, working with the Dark, manipulate these emotions into hatred, violence, and war. Unfortunately, not enough people are using the Sacred Fire to eliminate the resulting disturbance, so an equal measure such as war must be used to combat the violence. Violence, terrorism, torture, rape, and the like are terribly destructive to civilization's progress toward freedom and must be stopped.

I hope that in the future, we will need only the Sacred Fire to dissolve these hatred patterns within a person, thereby eliminating the threat of war. The Immortals use the Sacred Fire in periodic cleansings for the planet, but because we create our own reality as Divine Aspects of the I AM, we keep recreating the same discord over and over. The solution to war then is mortal everyday people using the Sacred Fire to purify themselves and their environment. Until then, we will have to use what tools we have. It is important for those who genuinely want peace and freedom not to be self-righteous toward those who are protecting our freedoms the best way they know how. Many spiritual liberals are very self-righteous and consider traditional people inferior. Spiritual liberalism has evolved out of the need to "fear god" and has often replaced it with arrogance. Many do not have a solid spiritual foundation and go from one belief to another allowing everything to be permissible. For all the good the New Age movement has produced, over the past 10 years there has been a cancer growing within her that is self-centered and full of arrogant meanness. If the New Age liberals continue on this course, they will self-destruct. Of course, this could be a good thing, since a rebirth from the ashes would bring a wiser and more mature, spiritual person.

Our leaders and teachers that we choose need to have a strong bedrock of spiritual values. Everyone is flawed, but it is important to judge a person by what they are doing now with their life. When confronted with past mistakes, if they openly and honestly admit those mistakes and have corrected them, we should accept that. Honesty, integrity, a strong belief in God, an understanding of right and wrong, and the courage to do the right thing are essential.

When we are young, most of us tend to be more liberal in our beliefs because we have not been taught universal laws. What morals we have are usually tied to fears and repression, so naturally we rebel. Our innate intelligence knows that we are free to choose our own way, but without proper guidance, that way is usually plunging into every sort of excess and addiction. Most of the time, age curbs this somewhat, but even as 40- and 50-year old adults, we are still being led around by our addictions. *This is why it is imperative that people in authority and with influence are as free as possible from addictions. Their values need to be conservative and based in as much spiritual devotion as possible.*

America has more people who believe in freedom incarnated within its borders than any country on Earth. We have used that freedom to create great material wealth, which is the first stage towards spiritual freedom. Once our material and emotional needs have been met, we can begin seeking a deeper meaning to life. Unfortunately, many people in the world do not have that freedom. The United States bears the greatest responsibility for the protection of freedom and Light for the world. *We must accept our responsibility and be willing to free those who are in darkness and oppression and provide material and spiritual support. Most importantly, we need to protect our country to ensure that spiritual freedom continues to flourish.*

When you begin to work with Universal Laws and understand that life is abundant and limitless, you realize there will always be enough to go around. Jesus fed thousands of people with only one loaf of bread and some fish. Americans are generous people, opening our hearts, giving of our prosperity and protection.

As the Immortals say, *without freedom-loving countries, the path to immortality could be lost.* We are the bridge between the Immortals and the rest of the world. While doing our duty to protect and support the world, we are also the trailblazers laying the path back to our immortal selves and into the Golden Age. The Immortals believe many people are ready for this information and if there is going to be any "mass" resurrections or ascensions, it will only happen if millions of people start embracing their true identity and let go of the world of seduction.

DESTINY

Destiny has finally found me,
Rising up a giant tower upon my path,
Large and immobile, it will not let me pass.
My knees go weak, as now the inevitable is upon me.

One thinks they are living a life true unto themselves, But this is not so.
It is only when the past, present, and future coalesce, in one defining moment—that you truly come alive.

I saw a man go through this recently, George
Bush, a man who was living a life he thought he
knew and understood—only to have destiny rise
up and meet him in the tragedy of 9-11.

This is how you know when you have met your destiny; there is nowhere you can run or hide,
For it is put upon you.
There is nothing I can do now,
Destiny has found me.
I shall raise my head high, stiffen my spine, and open my arms to embrace the moment.

I'm Schizophrenic and Half Crazed!

I'm tired of all the spats—think I'll become a Rebulocrat.
I'm split in two—what do I do?
I love nature and don't eat meat.
I believe in shrinking the government and being self-reliant,
Live and let Live—don't' ask don't tell.
Don't take my guns or you'll pay hell.
Help out my neighbor and the down-trodden.
I can't stand taxes.
There's no victim only opportunities.
We create our own reality.
Jesus rocks!
Yep—I teach Immortality.
I'm in the wrong time, in the wrong time.
I'm a Vulcan (like Topal) living among stinky humans.
Get up on your feet—dead beat!
I even rhyme half the time.
Is there no one in the world like
me half Christian—half New Ager?
Oh yeah—there's Arnold Schwarzenegger.

The Right & Left Become "Centered"

The greatest example of who we can be was demonstrated to us in the life and ascension of Jesus. I challenge the Christian Conservative Right and the New Age Liberal Left to come together and create a new world. Accepting our immortality is the first step in this process. We have everything to gain by having the courage to be free. Let us be the examples of the Right and the Left, at last...

"CENTERED"

Compassionate conservatism
Personal accountability liberalism
Honor and respect for *all* life including plants, animals, and the unborn child.
Self-reliance and personal responsibility
Doing to others as you would like others to do to you
Strong moral and spiritual convictions
Mental, emotional, and physical discipline
Joyful, free-flowing creativity and exploration
Patience and understanding
Courage and determination
A clean and healthy, mind, body, and environment

The absence of lust, greed, and corruption
No poverty, hunger, genocide, or abortions
The eliminations of addictions such alcohol, drugs, gambling, sexual lust, greed, and gluttony
The absence of soul-destroying stimuli such as pornography, violent, sexual, and sadistic music, movies and television
Truth, honesty, and integrity in all things
All for one and one for all
Synergistic oneness, we are all connected
What I do affects you and what you do affects me
The restoration of Jesus as the worlds spiritual leader
Cause and Effect, you reap as you have sown.
Face everything and avoid nothing
God included in all things including government and schools
The teaching of Universal Laws from childhood
The use of the Sacred Fire to cleanse away all discord
Progress with a conscience
Eliminating lack mentality
Eliminating victim status and the need to be rescued.

First, master yourself before
disciplining others
There is no such thing as a vengeful God
Love is all there is
Practice makes perfect
Only you can change your life, no one can
do it for you
Live and let live
Leaders and teachers who are the
best of humanity
Protect and defend freedom and liberty
The elimination of all separation
Telepathic communication with all
living things
Dematerialization and teleportation at will
All that we desire is produced instantly in
the material
Traveling to other worlds and dimensions
of light
The resurrection, immortality, and ascension
of humanity
Reunion with the Rays of Light, the
I AM Children
And the Great I AM.

GLOSSARY OF TERMS FOR STUDY

Aliens: Rays of Light or Separatist Rays of Light visiting Earth from other planets or systems.

Angels: Angels are Immortals from Earth or Rays of Light that have never taken on a physical body. Their general purpose is that of messenger, protector, or helper. The physical encounters that people have are usually *with* Immortals.

Ascended Masters: Those Immortals who have gone beyond the original body by shattering its blueprint using the Sacred Fire and merging with their Creator, the I AM Children, to create a new body. Ascended Masters can exist in both the worlds of Light and in the worlds of thought. Ascended Masters are the governing power for our planet and work with other Rays of Light and Counsels throughout the galaxy.

Ascension: The process whereby an Immortal activates a portion of the Sacred Fire and, using this Fire, shatters the old Separatist blueprint body both in the physical and energetic/thought realms. After that, the consciousness of the Immortal "ascends" into a new blueprint body created by the I AM Father. Other

Rays of Light who are ascended act as protectors as the old blueprint is being shattered and the new one anchored.

Astral Plane: See *Heaven/Hell*

Blueprint Body: The energetic blueprint of a form held together with thought-magnetism. This blueprint originates from the creative mind of the I AM, I AM Children, or Rays of Light. The more Rays of Light put their thoughts and feelings into a particular blueprint, the stronger and more resilient that blueprint becomes in the universe. The Separatist body became a very strong, energetic blueprint because of the Rays' strong attachment to the sensations it produced.

Creator: See *I AM Children*

Dark Brotherhood, Dark Forces: See *Separatist Rays of Light*

Dematerialization: A solid form that temporarily disappears from the visible light spectrum. In order for this to occur, an "innate intelligence" (i.e., Ray of Light) must be activating the process. During the process, the solid form's light particles begin to accelerate. This acceleration process increases the light quotient and the original form, held together with thought magnetism, is dissolved or raised into a higher light spectrum. To rematerialize the solid form, the opposite occurs, in that the light particles are decelerated or slowed down and moved back into the visible light spectrum.

Extraterrestrials: Rays of Light from other systems and planets. Many, *such as the Grays*, have become attached to their own type of physical body and are, therefore, part of the Separatists. Some, however, did not become attached to the physical form and can, therefore, release their form at will. Some have developed advanced inter-planetary spaceships for travel in order to carry their physical bodies long distances.

God: See *I AM Children*

Golden Age: This age is already occurring and available to anyone who wishes to follow in the footsteps of Jesus, Saint Germain, and others.

Heaven/Hell: Realms of light vibration where people go after they have shed the body and are waiting to reincarnate back into another physical body. These realms have many different kingdoms, each having its own government and society. These kingdoms are like life on Earth. How you lived your life on Earth will determine which kingdom you reside in while staying in these realms. Some of these realms are very hellish and filled with Dark Forces, while others are very spiritual and filled with people who love. Most people are somewhere in between, depending upon their addictions and ability to love.

I AM Children: The first act of the I AM to Know Himself in a more personal way was to create individual aspects of Himself known as, The I Am Children. They exist in the realms of thought, and their numbers are beyond infinity. They created the physical universes and all known patterns of Light. On Earth, we know them as God, God the Father, or the I AM Presence. The I AM Children gave birth to the Rays of Light, which inhabit the realms of Light. The I AM Children are the source of all life to the Rays of Light.

Immortals: Immortals are Rays of Light that have freed themselves from the world of the senses. No longer living in the Separatist illusion, their bodies naturally rejuvenate and become immortal. All that they desire is created instantly from thought. They live on Earth and are middle management between the Ascended Masters and humanity. They act as physical guardian angels and messengers for humanity in fulfilling the Ascended Masters' plans.

Jesus: A Ray of Light who was sent from his Father, one of the I AM Children, to incarnate into the Separatist body. He retained his true identity with the help of the Immortals and other non-corrupted Rays of Light. His purpose was to shatter or defeat the Separatist blueprint. After Jesus was crucified, he stood beside his body in spirit form and activated an aspect of the Sacred Fire, which restored and rejuvenated his body. Other Immortals were present during this process. Several months later, he went through an ascension process using the Sacred Fire. Before Jesus' ascension, many Immortals used advanced extraterrestrial technology and/or an aspect of the Sacred Fire to eliminate as much attachment to the Separatist body as possible. This gave the Immortals great freedom of movement and travel, even though they retained their original form. Jesus shattered the energetic blueprint permanently when the I AM Father descended into the immortal Jesus with a new energetic blueprint. This new design allowed Jesus and his Creator to exist as one, thereby creating a new type of Being, which not only existed in the realms of thought, but also in the realms of light.

Love: The source of all things, the essence of the I AM. Nothing exists that is *not* Love.

Magic: A craft the Separatists developed that uses the Powers of Nature and the Elementals to create and manipulate form, and events on

Earth. These powers and forces were originally created by the I AM Children and/or Rays of Light.

Nature Spirits/Elementals: Energetic blueprints created by the I AM Children or Rays of Light to assist in the creation of Earth. These energy blueprints were instilled with a limited consciousness designed for specific duties. They exist throughout the physical universe. Totally neutral, they are used by Rays of Light and Immortals for creating physical forms. The Separatists, however, have enslaved many of these spirits and have imposed their will upon them. An example of such nature spirits would be larvae, which attach to people in order to vampire their light.

Purgatory: See *Heaven/Hell*

Resurrection: An event that happens after a person or creature has died, whereupon the physical body is reanimated and returned to life. Magical resurrections use borrowed light from the Astral/Earthly realms. This light eventually exhausts itself, thereby terminating the life. Resurrections using the Sacred Fire totally restore and rejuvenate the body.

Retreats: Dwelling places of the Immortals on Earth. They are usually located in remote mountainous areas, underwater locations, or inside the Earth. Some of the retreats exist at a slightly higher vibration than our visible eyes can detect. Others are located within our cities and countrysides around the world.

Sacred Fire: The pure, incorruptible essence of the I AM given to humanity from the I AM Children. The Fire can only be activated by a person's freewill, which when called upon and accepted, gives its gifts and powers. There are many aspects of the Sacred Fire. One that is well known is the Violet Flame, which is used to cleanse and purify a person's discordant energy and eliminate their human addictions. Other aspects of the Fire are healing, realigning energy fields, protection, teleportation, direct manifestation, restoration of youth, immortalizing the body, and activating ascension. A future book will go into more detail concerning the use of the Sacred Fire.

Separatist Rays of Light: Those offspring of the I AM Children who over identified with their physical form and its sensations. They lost the memory of who they were and became trapped in the illusion of form. The Rays who are attached the *most* to sensations are known on Earth as the Dark Forces, Dark Brotherhood, or Evil. However, everyone who incarnates on Earth and is not already an Immortal is a Separatist.

Soul Mates: These are Rays of Light or people who have spent many lifetimes together and have become familiar with each other's behaviors and addictions. Each person may have many soul mates.

Saint Germain: An Ascended Master who was known during his immortal life as the Comte de Saint Germain, and the Wonderman of Europe. He is mentioned in the memoirs of many of the Royals in Europe. Saint Germain conceived and brought about the establishment of the United States of America. He worked with the "Founding Fathers" and inspired many of our historical documents. He also assisted George Washington and many other Presidents. He is the Ascended Master known as the Master of Freedom and works tirelessly to preserve freedom everywhere in the world. America is beloved by him.

The I AM: The One, the Source, Love. There is nothing that is not the I AM.

Thought-Magnetism: Every structure or form in the Light universes is held together by an original thought or desire. This thought is a magnetic energy, which draws together the substance needed to create the thought or idea into matter or solid form.

Twin Rays of Light: The offspring of the I AM Children in the worlds of light and matter. One Twin Ray is predominantly reflective and resting while, the other is active and creative. They are known on Earth as Humanity.

Violet Flame: A portion of the Sacred Fire used to dissolve a person's negative creations and addictions. It is used in the retreats by the Immortals. In the 1930s, Saint Germain gave this information to Guy Ballard to share with humanity in a series of books known as the *Saint Germain Books.* (See Suggested Reading Material)

Suggested Reading Material & Sources

Unveiled Mysteries and *The Magic Presence* by Godfre Ray King, Saint Germain Press, Schaumburg, Illinois, 800-662-2800. This two-volume series tells the story of a man who met the Ascended Master Saint Germain, who immortalized his body, and later ascended. The books describe the history of Earth, ascension, and the use of the Violet Flame and the I AM.

The Saint Germain Volumes Three–Eighteen, edited by The Saint Germain Press, Schaumburg, Illinois, 800-622-2800. Further insight on the use of the Violet Flame and the I AM by various Immortal Beings.

Autobiography of a Yogi by Paramahansa Yogananda, Self- Realization Fellowship, Los Angeles, California. This is a true story of an Indian Yogi's remarkable experiences including meetings with the Immortal Babaji. Yogananda took these teachings to America and established the Self- Realization Fellowship.

Babaji and the Eighteen Siddha Kriya Yogic Tradition by Marshall Govindan, published by Kriya Yoga Publications, Canada. This book tells the story of many of the Immortals from India including Babaji.

Life and Teaching of the Masters of the Far East Vols. 1–
5, by Baird Spalding, Devorss and Co, Marina del Rey, California. This is the story of an archeologist who goes on an expedition to India and meets with great Immortals who demonstrate many miraculous abilities.

The Way Out by Anonymous, author of *The Impersonal*
Life, DeVorss and Co., Marina del Rey, California. A wonderful little book packed with great wisdom. Following the suggestions in this book will definitely set you on the path to immortality.

The Comte de St. Germain- The Secret of Kings, by I. Cooper Oakley, Book Tree Publishing. This is the historical account of the great Immortal, The Comte de Saint Germain, who immortalized his body through alchemical processes and later ascended. This account is taken directly from the memoirs of many of the royal houses in Europe who knew Saint Germain personally. They called him, "The Wonderman of Europe."

The Most Holy Trinosophia by Comte De St. Germain, Philosophical Research Society Inc., Los Angeles, California. This work is the alchemical description of Saint Germain's immortalization process written in his own words.

Embracing Heaven and Earth: The Liberation Teachings by Andrew Cohen, Moksha Press, Larkspur, California. Andrew Cohen gives the student practical steps to free themselves from self-centeredness and embrace enlightenment.

What is Enlightenment? A magazine published by Andrew Cohen, Contact information: 888-837-7739 or *www.wie.org.* This wonderful quarterly magazine discusses enlightenment and its various forms and expressions.

SOURCES

The St. Germain Foundation - Contact information: 800-662-2800. This foundation has study groups actively working on ascension in every state and country. These groups hold weekly meetings to work with the Violet Flame and to study the series of books written by Godfre Ray King (see Suggested Reading Material and Sources section). This is, by far, the best group of people I have ever met. The foundation is extremely dedicated to the pursuit of ascension, and the people are very honorable, caring, and the *best* possible avenue for working on letting go of your addictions.

Andrew Cohen's Fellowship and Ashrams - Contact information: 800-376-3210, 413-637-6000 or *www.andrewcohen.org,* Lenox MA. Andrew Cohen has a few ashrams; his primary ones are in Boston and Lenox, MA. The fellowship accepts members who are truly dedicated to releasing their self-centeredness and are willing to devote their lives to the pursuit of true spiritual freedom and enlightenment. This is the only ashram I can recommend. Andrew is an honorable teacher and his students are wonderful people. I have attended some of his workshops and I highly recommend them.

About the Author

✠ The author, Jhershierra, was born with several spiritual gifts. She has the ability to travel out-of-body and/or be conscious in the Heavenly/Astral worlds. These abilities have given her access to great Beings and the opportunity to be an active participant in those realms.

✠ Immortals, Ascended Masters, Extraterrestrials, and other Spiritual Beings have visited Jhershierra since childhood.

✠ Jhershierra is a planetary channel for the Sacred Fire. Using the Fire, she has performed healings, exorcisms, energy realignments, and Sacred Fire activations, to name a few.

✠ In the 1980s, after being in the healthcare field, Jhershierra left to pursue a more spiritual path. In Texas, she co-owned a small newspaper called *Insights for Positive Living* and a bookstore/center called, "The Souls Journey." She taught classes on various spiritual topics including immortality at the center.

✠ In the 1990s, Jhershierra moved to Colorado where she continued to teach classes in the

United States and Europe on ascension and immortality.

- ✠ In the late 1990s, Jhershierra took a sabbatical from public teaching and pursued organic gardening and further development of the Sacred Fire.
- ✠ Currently, Jhershierra lives in Texas where she teaches the path to immortality.

CONTACT INFORMATION FOR:

Jhershierra

Website: *www.jhershierra.com*
Email: *info@jhershierra.com*

Jhershierra is available for lectures, workshops, and book signings. She is also available for healings, exorcisms, and Sacred Fire activations on a case-by-case basis.

To order the book online:

www.booklocker.com

www.amazon.com

www.bn.com (Barnes and Noble)

Wholesale orders of this book are available through Ingram and New Leaf Distributors.

Printed in the United States
26317LVS00001B/462